HORRIBLE HISTORIES

AWESOME EGYPTIANS

TERRY DEARY & PETER HEPPLEWHITE

ILLUSTRATED BY MARTIN BROWN

Scholastic Canada Ltd.

Toronto New York London Auckland Sydney

Mexico City New Delhi Hong Kong Buenos Aires

Scholastic Canada Ltd.
604 King Street West, Toronto, Ontario M5V 1E1, Canada

Scholastic Inc.
557 Broadway, New York, NY 10012, USA

Scholastic Australia Pty Limited
PO Box 579, Gosford, NSW 2250, Australia

Scholastic New Zealand Limited
Private Bag 94407, Greenmount, Auckland, New Zealand

Scholastic Children's Books
Euston House, 24 Eversholt Street, London NW1 1DB, UK

Library and Archives Canada Cataloguing in Publication

Deary, Terry
Awesome Egyptians / Terry Deary, author ; Martin Brown, illustrator.

(Horrible histories)
ISBN 978-0-545-99785-0

1. Egypt--Civilization--To 332 B.C.--Juvenile literature. I. Brown,
Martin, 1959- II. Title. III. Series: Deary, Terry. Horrible histories
DT61.D42 2007   j932   C2007-902228-6

ISBN-10: 0-545-99785-2

Text copyright © Terry Deary and Peter Hepplewhite 1993, 2007
Illustrations © Martin Brown, 1993, 2007
First published in the U.K. by Scholastic Ltd., 1993.
First Canadian edition published 2007.
All rights reserved.

6 5 4 3   Printed in Canada   09 10 11

CONTENTS

Introduction

Math lessons are full of problems . . . but English lessons are quite another story. Music lessons can break all records . . . but Geography lessons have their ups and downs. Chemistry lessons can be a gas . . . but Biology lessons are full of life.

P.E. lessons are one long game . . . but History!

History is **horrible**! Horrible dates to remember, horrible kings fighting horrible battles against horrible people. Sometimes it all gets horribly boring!

Sometimes history can be horribly unfair!

Sometimes it can be horribly confusing!

But this book is about **really horrible** history. The sort of thing that teachers never tell you! Teachers don't always tell you the whole truth! Honestly!

Teachers think you're too young to learn about gruesome things . . . like the way Egyptians took the brains out of their mummies! So they don't tell you . . . then you leave school, and you may never ever learn this vital information.

And sometimes teachers don't tell you things because they don't know the facts themselves! (That's right! Teachers do not know everything . . . just some teachers *think* they do.)

So, this book will tell you the things teachers won't. And by the time you're finished you will be able to teach your teacher . . . you'll enjoy that!

In this book, you'll find lots of other interesting things:

. . .stories to make your blood run colder than a crocodile's claw!

. . .things to do that will be more fun than eating a bag of chips under water!

. . .facts that are funnier than a teacher's joke, nastier than a tramp's sock or sadder than a three-legged sheep. I hope you'll find them all horrible fun!

Egypt factfile

The most awesome fact about the Egyptians was that their civilization lasted an awfully long time—over 3,000 years. They had been around so long that their monuments were ancient even in Greek and Roman times.

Timeline of important events

Egyptian time is usually measured in periods called dynasties. A dynasty was the length of time that a ruling family lasted. Each dynasty could have as many as fourteen kings in the family . . . or as few as one. There were 30 Egyptian dynasties altogether, followed by two Greek ones, before Egypt finally fell to the Romans and then the Arabs. This is an awesomely quick race through time. . .

Awesome Egyptian events

Time: 3200–2300 B.C.
Dynasty: 1–6
Period: The Old Kingdom

Events: Upper and Lower Egypt joined together and Nile floods controlled by drain-building.

Hieroglyphic writing in common use by scribes, and calendar invented.

The first pyramids built, including the Great Pyramid of Cheops.

Time: 2300–2050 B.C.
Dynasty: 7–11
Period: First Intermediate Period

Events: Weak rule by Pepy leads to revolution and mob violence.

Starvation for many peasants.

Time: 2050–1775 B.C.
Dynasty: 11–12
Period: The Middle Kingdom

Events: Clever Pharaohs.
Art, craft and writing very rich with huge temples being built and decorated.
First bakeries in the world started in Egypt.

Time: 1775–1575 B.C.
Dynasty: 13–17
Period: Second Intermediate Period

Events: "Shepherd Kings"— invaders from Asia— rule the North.
Horses and chariots beginning to be used.
First sweets in the world made in Egypt.
Better spinning and weaving. New musical instruments such as oboe and tambourine.

9

Time: 1575–1085 B.C.
Dynasty: 18–20
Period: The New Kingdom

Events: "Shepherd Kings" thrown out.

The greatest period in Ancient Egypt's history.

Rock tombs in the Valley of the Kings started.

Tutankhamun lived and died.

Rameses II fights Hittites in great battle at Kadesh.

Book of the Dead written on papyrus.

Hebrew slaves in Egypt led to freedom by Moses.

Time: 1085–709 B.C.
Dynasty: 21–24
Period: The Decadence Period

Events: Gradual end of the Egyptian kings.

Egypt has to use soldiers from Libya to fight its battles.

Time: 709–332 B.C.
Dynasty: 25–30
Period: The Late Period

Events: Egypt invaded by Assyrians.

Egypt led by Persian Kings.

Nubian rulers are first people to encourage the study of history.

Time: 332–30 B.C.
Period: The Ptolemaic Period

Event: Egypt conquered by Alexander the Great of Greece.

Ruled by the Ptolemy family Greeks.

Last Queen of Egypt was Cleopatra.

Time: 30 B.C.
Events: Egypt part of the Roman Empire.

Egypt is used to supply food to the Roman World.

Time: 641 A.D.
Events: Egypt conquered by the Arabs.

Phascinating Pharaohs

The most awesome sight that you can see in Egypt is the pyramids. And the most awesome things that you can't see are the people who had them built—the Egyptian kings, or Pharaohs. They've now turned to dust, bones, musky mummies and, of course, history. But how did they come about?

Before Egypt was a country, small villages had grown up on the banks of the Nile River. Each village had a chief. The most powerful chiefs took over other villages from neighbouring chiefs. They became kings of small kingdoms by the Nile.

Again, the most powerful would conquer neighbours and become even more powerful. In the end there were just two awesome chiefs—the King of Upper Egypt with his white crown and the King of Lower Egypt with his red crown.

About 3200 B.C., King Menes of Upper Egypt conquered Lower Egypt—he joined the two crowns as a symbol. The country we now know as ancient Egypt was born.

Villages with chiefs changed to countries with kings in a matter of only 200 years. How could this change have happened so quickly? Some historians think the new leaders were an awesomely clever group of people from outside Egypt—conquerors in fact. There is proof that these early kings were taller and had much larger heads than the peasants of Egypt!

One leading historian says they came from the East. A leading hysteric says they must have come

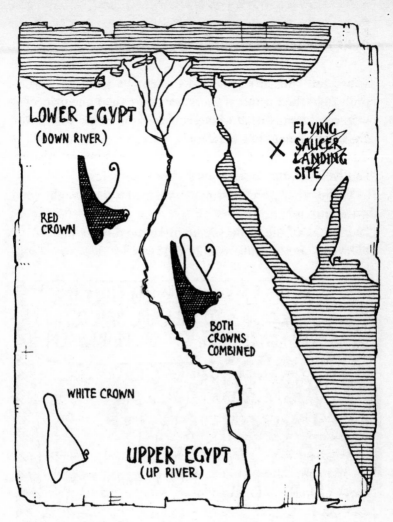

LOWER EGYPT
(DOWN RIVER)

RED
CROWN

BOTH
CROWNS
COMBINED

WHITE CROWN

UPPER EGYPT
(UP RIVER)

× FLYING
SAUCER
LANDING
SITE

from another planet. Their skeletons and their graves have been found . . . their flying saucer has not. Still, no one is certain . . . *make up your own mind*. In any case, wherever they came from, it was their even more awesome descendants who built the pyramids.

Could you have been an Egyptian king?

To become king, first you had to marry a princess whose family held the throne. If there was more than one princess in the royal family what would you do? How could you make sure that *you* would be the king?

A Kill all the other princesses except your wife?
B Let the other princesses marry men who might fight you for the throne?
C Marry *all* of the princesses to make the throne safe?
D Have the other princesses locked away?

Answer: C was the most common. There was no limit to the number of wives a king could have. The more royal princesses he could marry, the safer he would be.

Your royal role

As a king, here are some of your duties. . .

The Heb-sed festival
Are you fit? The king has to prove his fitness by running around a fixed course. This is usually held after the king has ruled for 30 years. This terrible trial is held at the Heb-sed festival.

Religious leader
Remember you are not just a king; you are also a god. Every morning the king has to make offerings to the other gods. This is to ask the sun to rise. If you don't, then the sun won't rise and the world will end! (If you are a bit lazy, don't worry. The priests usually do this job for you—the priests will also eat the offerings to the gods as part of their payment.) One of your other powers is command over the great Nile River. Each year you perform the ceremonies to make the river rise and flood the land. This keeps the land fertile for growing crops, and the people well fed.

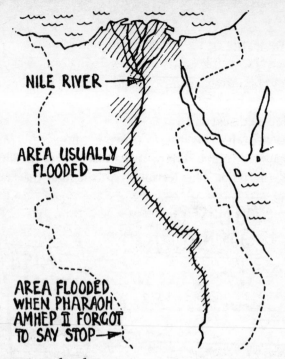

NILE RIVER

AREA USUALLY FLOODED →

AREA FLOODED WHEN PHARAOH AMHEP II FORGOT TO SAY STOP →

Government leader

An important duty is to keep the two parts of Egypt together—Upper and Lower Egypt. Feeling a bit overwhelmed? Don't worry, you have lots of officials to help you run the country.

The royal nickname

Of course, it's very unlikely you would have been an Egyptian king, and much more likely you'd have been a commoner. As a commoner you'd have to mind your manners with the king. For a start, you'd be in big trouble if you called the king...well..."King!" If you were an ordinary Egyptian it could mean death. The Egyptians believed that their ruler was sacred. They were supposed to be in awe of him. After all, he wasn't just a king, but a god as well. So

16

it was very insulting to use his private name! Instead they used respectful nicknames. The most popular nickname was Pharaoh, which meant "Great House" or "Palace"—because the king's body was the human "house" of a god.

Awesome army leader

The carvings on all Egyptian monuments show the king as a conqueror. What if you lose? Don't worry, the writers (scribes) can still say you won! Rameses II fought the Hittites at the Battle of Qadesh in Syria—the Egyptian scribes described his great victory. The Hittite writers described the same battle—but in the Hittite story the Hittites won!

Is she a queen ... or a king?

The king of Egypt was a man ... but occasionally he could be a woman. Yes, a woman could be a king! If a woman was the most powerful person in Egypt then she would rule the kingdom ... but the Egyptians would never see her as a queen.

For the king of Egypt was also the son of the chief god, Re. The son of Re had to be a man, didn't he? So, the king had to be a man even if she was a woman, see! If she didn't have the qualities of a man then the Egyptians gave them to her. She would have to have a beard ... so they gave her a chin wig.

I WOULDN'T LOOK UP THERE IF I WERE YOU

Hatshepsut was a woman-king, and she often dressed in men's clothes to look the part. She had her name written on monuments all over Egypt. But the kings that followed Hatshepsut were so confused, and in awe of her, they scratched her name off the monuments again. They tried to pretend that woman-king Hatshepsut had never existed.

Cleopatra was the most famous Queen of Egypt, and she didn't have to pretend to be a man. However, she ruled the country almost 1,500 years after Hatshepsut—and she was a foreigner: a Greek.

The terrible tragedy of Tutankhamun ... or, Would you marry your grandfather?

King Akhenaten was a problem. He had a crazy idea that there was only one god in Egypt, Aten. And he spent so much time bothering about Aten that he forgot to defend Egypt against its enemies. The chief ministers must have been frantic.

King Akhenaten had to go. And he went. He died suddenly and mysteriously. His Uncle Ay, the highest minister, probably had something to do with it. He saw to it that Akhenaten's younger brother, Tutankhamun, became the new king. He was only nine when he took over the throne so he couldn't sort out Egypt's problems by himself. So his Uncle Ay helped him out ... and helped himself to an awesome amount of power.

Uncle Ay sorted out the religion problems and the defence of the country. In fact, Uncle Ay ran the country while young Tutankhamun lived a quieter life with his wife, Ankhesenamun. They were very fond of hunting.

Then Tutankhamun died. How? He could have died of natural causes ... but he was only eighteen. Or was he *murdered?* Maybe Tutankhamun had decided it was time to take over from Uncle Ay ... and maybe Uncle Ay didn't want to let go of the power he'd enjoyed for nearly ten years.

There were only two ways that Uncle Ay could hang on to that power. He could fight for it ... but he might lose in battle. Or he could kill Tutankhamun and marry the boy-king's widow, Ankhesenamun ... but she was his granddaughter.

Ankhesenamun didn't like the idea of marrying her grandfather one little bit . . . would you? But what could she do? What would *you* have done if you'd been Ankhesenamun?

1. OFFER TO MARRY A FOREIGN PRINCE WHO WOULD BECOME THE NEW KING OF EGYPT?

2. POISON YOURSELF?

3. MARRY YOUR GRANDFATHER AND STAY AS QUEEN?

4. RUN AWAY?

Ankhesenamun chose number 1—I think I would have, too. She offered to marry Prince Zennanza, the son of the Hittite king, even though the Hittites were Egypt's enemies! The Hittite king sent Prince Zennanza to marry Ankhesenamun . . . but the prince never arrived! He was murdered on the way. And we can guess who arranged that!

After her plan failed Ankhesenamun agreed to marry Grandfather Ay. And the good news? Ay became king, but he only lived another four years. That probably served him right!

Kingly kuriosities...

1 King Pepy II ruled from the age of nine till he was over 100—awesomely longer than any other Egyptian king.

2 King Sneferu invited twenty of his wives to row across the palace lake to entertain him. It was going well when one wife dropped her hair clip into the water. She sulked and refused to go on. The king pleaded. She refused. Finally King Sneferu had to order the court magician to find it. An ancient story says that he folded one half of the lake on top of the other and found the hair clip.

3 Many kings hired magicians. One knew how to cut off a goose's head and replace it without harming the bird. Was this a bit like the sawing-a-lady-in-half trick of modern magicians? Another one could make a wild lion as tame as a pet.

WHY COULDN'T HE PULL ME OUT OF A HAT LIKE OTHER MAGICIANS

4 King Rameses II faced the Hittite army with no help but his pet lion . . . and lived! He prayed to the god Amun for help. At that moment an army of allies turned up and attacked the Hittites from the back. The enemy were driven into the river where many drowned. The Hittite king agreed to make peace with Rameses . . . and the lion.

5 The kings didn't just need their mummified bodies in the afterlife. They also needed their servants. Scribes and cooks and tailors and builders and . . . every servant they ever had on Earth. Most kings were buried with models of the servants they would need.

But the first few kings had a much more gruesome answer to the afterlife servant problem . . . when they died they took their human servants with them. The servants couldn't travel to the afterlife while they were still alive, so they had to be killed!

We don't know if they died willingly or had to be brutally murdered. We do know that outside King Zer's tomb, for example, there are the graves of 338 servants who were sacrificed at his funeral. It wasn't until the eighth king, Ka'a, was buried that this "awesome" custom died out.

Serving the king was a great honour. But would you like to have worked for him knowing that when he died, you died?

6   The Romans ruled Egypt as part of the Roman Empire. The days of the great kingdom of Egypt were ended after over 3,000 years. Ancient Egypt had been the longest-running empire in the history of humankind. Awesome!

7   The last kings of Egypt weren't Egyptian, they were all Greek. After Alexander the Great conquered the country in 332 B.C., the Greek Ptolemy family ruled the country for almost 300 years. The last Ptolemy ruler was awesome Queen Cleopatra. But Cleo came to a nasty end.

Cleopatra's lover was the Roman ruler, Julius Caesar. He had protected her from a Roman invasion—but Julius was then murdered. She had to decide which of his two successors she should support . . . Augustus or Mark Antony? She decided to bet on Mark Antony . . . and became *his* lover.

She lost her bet. And when Mark Antony lost in a war against Augustus—Cleo was finished. The end would have been hilarious if it hadn't been so tragic.

Mark Antony heard that Cleopatra had killed herself. He was so upset he fell on his sword and tried to kill *himself*. He failed.

Then he heard that Cleopatra *hadn't* tried to kill herself. She was alive! He had himself carried to her . . . then he died of his wound. Cleopatra was so upset she then really did kill herself.

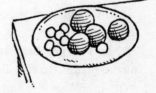

The power of the pyramids

12 August 1799

He was an awesome ruler—the most powerful in the world at that time. Now this great ruler of the new world had come to visit a great ruler of the ancient world. He was the leader of France, the conqueror of Europe. His name was Napoleon Bonaparte. Napoleon had come to the Pyramid of Cheops in Egypt.

His guide led him deeper and deeper into the heart of the ancient pyramid. At last they stood in the very centre of the King's Chamber. The guide began to explain what he knew about its history, but Napoleon silenced the man with a wave of his hand.

"Leave me alone," he said . . . in French.

"But, sir. . ."

"Alone!"

"As you wish, sir," the guide muttered and backed out of the chamber into the dark passageway. Napoleon was alone in the warm, still, silent air. It seemed a long time before the great man came out. The guide held up the lantern. Napoleon was pale and shaking.

"Is something wrong, sir?" the guide asked.

Napoleon seemed to ignore him. Then suddenly he said in a harsh, dry voice, "Do not ever mention this matter again!"

"No, sir," the guide muttered and led the way back into the dry, white heat of the Egyptian plain.

But later in his eventful life it was Napoleon who mentioned the visit. And he hinted—just hinted that he had experienced incredible things while he was inside that pyramid. Perhaps, he suggested, he had even seen a vision of his own future.

Then, when he lay dying on the island of St. Helena, he seemed about to tell his secret at last to a friend. "But no," he said weakly. "What is the use? You'd never believe me!"

He died shortly after. The mystery of the pyramid's power went to the grave with him.

The magic of the pyramid

One thousand years before Napoleon entered the King's Chamber, another great leader had stood in the same spot. His name was Al Mamun, the Caliph of Baghdad. Al Mamun was a young man and a very curious one. He'd heard about the magical powers of the pyramids and he wanted to find out for himself just what was inside one.

Most of the pyramids had been raided by grave robbers. They were empty. But no one had broken through the massive defences of the Pyramid of Cheops—known to this day as the Great Pyramid.

A King's Chamber had been dug deep into the rock under the Great Pyramid—perhaps to give a safe resting place for the king in case he died before the pyramid was finished. Another chamber had been designed for his queen. Finally, there was a chamber deep in the heart of the pyramid.

Once the coffin was in the chamber the passageways had been sealed with hard, granite blocks. When Al Mamun reached the Great Pyramid he found that no robbers had broken through the great blocks. But the young Caliph was determined . . . and he had an army of men to work for him.

They dug new tunnels through the rocks. At last they reached the centre. Al Mamun now entered. He'd heard the legends about the mysteries the pyramids contained. Ancient charts that showed the movement of the stars . . . maps of the world as the Egyptians knew it . . . pure metals and gold . . . and magical things like unbreakable glass.

In the centre of the King's chamber stood a stone coffin. And in the stone coffin was . . . nothing!

King Cheops had never been placed in this vast stone tomb. Why not? If it wasn't to be his burial place, then why was it built?

It's a mystery which has never been solved to this day. Maybe the answer is very simple—perhaps King Cheops was buried somewhere else because the pyramid wasn't ready in time. But for many people, that answer is too simple.

Dozens of people have put forward ideas . . . some more amazing than others.

If the Great Pyramid isn't a tomb, then why was it built? What else could a pyramid be? Which suggestion do you like best. . .?

29

Some awesome ideas about the pyramids

1 The Great Pyramid is a stone computer—if you take the lengths of the sides, and their heights and angles, you can calculate many different things. The pyramid will tell you how to work out the distance around the outside of a circle if you know the distance across it.

2 The Egyptians could use the Great Pyramid to work out the distance the Earth travels around the sun, and the speed of light.

3 The pyramid is a mathematical horoscope—you can calculate the future from it. The Institute of Pyramidology in London says the pyramid has already predicted the Crucifixion of Jesus and the First World War. It has also predicted that the world will end in the year 2979 A.D.

4 The Great Pyramid is a sign to the world how much knowledge the Egyptian priests had—and how much power. They persuaded Cheops to have it built and made him pay all the bills. Then when he died they didn't want his body inside their wonderful creation.

5 The Great Pyramid is an observatory for watching and recording the movements of the stars.

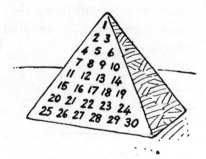

6 The Great Pyramid is a giant calendar. The Egyptians could use it to measure the length of a year to three decimal places.

7 The Great Pyramid is a sundial. The shadow fell on pavements and the pavements were marked with the day of the year and the hour of the day.

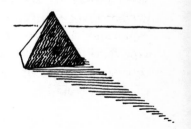

8 The Great Pyramid is a landmark. All ancient maps could use it as the starting point for drawing and measuring their charts, rather like the Greenwich Meridian is today.

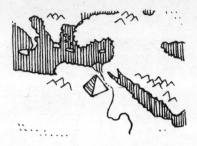

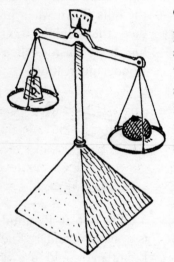

9 The Great Pyramid is a perfect store for the weights and measures of the ancient world. The government needed a master set of weights to check if traders were giving proper value when they sold goods. But weights like the *deben* were made of copper and lost weight after a few years' wear and tear—sometimes they were even "fixed" by crooked shopkeepers.

10 The centre of the pyramid is the centre of tremendous forces of nature. Strange and wonderful things can happen there . . . apart from Napoleon's very strange experience, many tourists have gone into shock or fainted when they reached the centre.

32

The powerful pyramid shape

Fifty years after Napoleon experienced the power of the Great Pyramid, another Frenchman called Bovis visited the great tomb. It was a mess. Other visitors had left rubbish lying around. A stray cat had wandered in and died—it was lying amongst the rubbish, forgotten. But Bovis noticed something strange about the body of the cat. It had not rotted as you'd expect. In fact it was so well preserved it could have been a mummy . . . but a mummy without any wrapping or embalming. Bovis decided that only one thing could have preserved the cat in this way . . . the power of the pyramid.

ZIS IZ VRRY STRARNGE

33

You've probably seen the way a magnifying glass can pull together the rays of the sun into one tiny, hot spot. Bovis decided that in the same way some powerful forces of nature are pulled together by the shape of the pyramid.

He went back to France and tried some experiments. He made model pyramids and placed different types of food inside them—food that usually turns bad in a very short time. He found that all the food stayed in good condition for much longer than anyone would expect!

Over a hundred years later, in 1959, an engineer from Czechoslovakia read about Bovis's experiments. His name was Karel Drbal. He wondered if the pyramid would preserve metal the way it preserved food. Razor blades were in short supply in his country in those days. So he put blunt blades under a model pyramid to see if it would stop them getting any blunter. To his astonishment, Drbal found that they actually became sharp again.

This was a great discovery. Drbal had to make sure the idea was not stolen by someone else. He needed a government patent that would allow Drbal to claim the idea was his alone. So Drbal went to the government Patent Office.

But when Drbal went back the next week the Chief Officer was a shaken man.

And Drbal sold the idea to a company who went on, very successfully, to make plastic models of pyramids and sell them as blade-sharpeners. The people of Czechoslovakia bought the plastic pyramids. They really believed that they worked.

But do you?

The Great Pyramid experiment

The best way to find out is to try your own Great Pyramid experiment.

1   Make a pyramid of cardboard—four triangles. The bottomless base of each triangle must be 15.7 centimetres (or 15.7 inches) and each side must be 14.94 centimetres (or 14.94 inches).

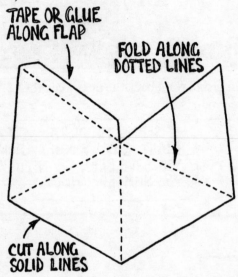

TAPE OR GLUE ALONG FLAP

FOLD ALONG DOTTED LINES

CUT ALONG SOLID LINES

2   Place a piece of bread or cheese or any other food in a small block so it is raised 3.33 centimetres (or 3.33 inches) off the base.

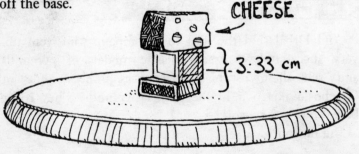

CHEESE

3.33 cm

3 Put the pyramid over the food so the food is in the centre.

4 Line up the pyramid so the sides face exactly north, south, east and west.

5 Have an identical piece of food outside the pyramid. Check the food each day.

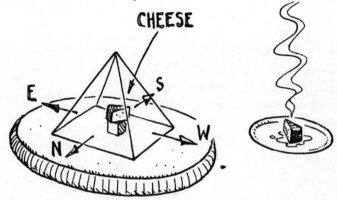

CHEESE

Which one goes stale or mouldy first? If you find the food inside the pyramid stays fresher, then maybe you have proved the power of the pyramid for yourself!

Did you know. . .?
There is an old soldiers' story from World War I (1914–1918). It was said that if you leave a razor blade out in the moonlight then it will go blunt. The edge of a razor is made up of tiny crystals that give a blade its sharpness. The pressure of the moonlight is enough to rub those fine crystals off. Could the forces inside a pyramid preserve the crystals in some way . . . the same way they preserve food, or the body of a dead Egyptian cat?

The pyramids

Ten awesome things you ought to know about the pyramids

1 A pyramid was supposedly built as the huge stone tomb of a Pharaoh (Egyptian king).

2 The pyramids were built from enormous stone blocks but no one is quite sure how the Egyptians moved the stones when they had no wheeled transport. And how did they lift them when they had no cranes?

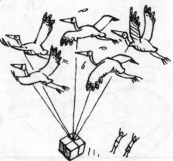

3 The burial chamber in the centre was filled with awesome riches for the Pharaoh to take to the afterlife.

4 The riches were a temptation to robbers. The pyramid builders tried to fool the thieves by making false doors, staircases and corridors.

5 The base of the Great Pyramid of Cheops is equal to the area of seven or eight football pitches (230 metres by 230 metres).

6 The burial chamber inside the Great Pyramid is as large as a small modern house (ten metres by five metres and six metres high).

7 The pyramids are close to the Nile because some of the huge stones had to be carried from the quarries by boat.

8 The pyramids are all on the west bank of the Nile—the side on which the sun sets. This is for religious reasons.

9   The Pharaohs were buried with religious writings to help them in the afterlife. The earliest ones were written on the walls of the burial chambers (they're called the Pyramid Texts.) Later they were written on the coffins (the Coffin Texts.) The last were written on Egyptian paper (papyrus) and rolled up and placed in the dead man's coffin. The writings described different ways to get to the afterworld and are known as the Books of the Dead.

10   The Ancient Greeks visited the pyramids as tourists. They reported that each pyramid had taken 100,000 slaves ten years to build. Some modern history books still repeat these facts, yet they are almost certainly wrong in every respect. The workers were free craftsmen, not slaves, and it probably took just 70,000 to 80,000 men five years to finish a pyramid. They were paid partly in radishes and garlic, which helped keep them healthy.

Test your tyrant ... er ... teacher...

Teachers don't know everything! Awesome—but true! Try your teacher with these true-or-false questions. If they get all nine right, they're a genius!

True or false?

1   Mummies were sometimes buried with model dolls.

2   Wood was a precious material in Egypt because trees were scarce. This is one of the reasons why the Egyptians were so good at building in stone.

3   The Egyptians are thought to have dragged the stones on sledges to the early pyramids because they hadn't invented the wheel.

4   Some Pharaohs were buried with a Book of the Dead called *The Book of the Divine Cow.*

5   Pyramids as burial places went out of fashion for almost a thousand years between 1800 B.C. and 800 B.C.

6 Pyramids contained everything the king would need in the afterlife . . . including a toilet.

7 The Step Pyramid at Saqqara was the first large stone building the world had ever seen.

8 The Great Pyramid is made of about 2,300,000 stone blocks.

9 There are over 90 pyramids in Egypt.

Answer: All the above statements are TRUE!

Ancient Egyptian ancient joke

Ten things you'll probably never need to know about pyramids...

1 If you broke the Great Pyramid into slabs 30 centimetres thick you could build a wall one metre high that would stretch all the way around France. If you had a little more time you could cut the stone into rods about six centimetres square—join them together and you'd have enough to reach the Moon!

2 Some people have said that the pyramids are more than simply large graves; they were granaries or treasure houses.

3 All of the pyramids were probably robbed of their treasures within a couple of hundred years of the burials. The only tombs to escape until modern times were those dug into rock, not placed in pyramids. They belonged to Tutankhamun and Queen Hetepheres.

4 The Egyptians mummified more than their Pharaohs. They mummified the Pharaohs' pets and buried them in the pyramids to keep the dead kings company.

5 If you could weigh an average pyramid it would be around 5,400,000 tonnes. The average stone block weighs as much as two modern cars (2.5 tonnes). The largest single stone block (in the Pyramid of Mycerinus) must weigh about 285 tonnes—that's 200 to 250 cars.

6 Pyramid-builders tried to fool thieves by placing a blocking stone at the end of a passageway and plastering it in. If the thieves broke through the plaster then they would come to the stone and give up. The real way into the tomb would then be through a hidden trapdoor in the ceiling.

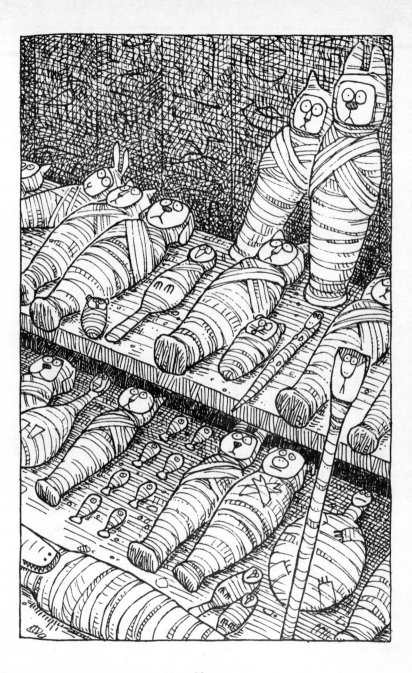

43

7 The Egyptians didn't have accurate metal tape measures. They used fibre cords which could shrink or stretch. Still, the greatest mistake in the Great Pyramid is just 20 centimetres on a side of 230 metres (an error of less than 0.1 per cent). They were even more accurate in building a flat base—the south-east corner is just one centimetre higher than the north-west corner.

8 The pyramids are not the most awesomely large human construction. The Great Wall of China is much more awesome and the Mexican Pyramid of Quetzacoatl is an even more awesome 54 metres tall and has a volume of 3.3 million cubic metres. The Great Pyramid of Cheops is just 2.5 million cubic metres. But the pyramids of Egypt are the *oldest* stone buildings in the world.

9 Early tombs were flat-topped. These were called Mastabas because they looked like the mud-brick seat found outside Egyptian peasant homes. Mastaba tombs were easily robbed. So someone built a slightly smaller Mastaba on top of the first one . . . then another on top of that . . . and then another . . . and they ended up with a "step" pyramid.

10 It is forbidden to climb the pyramids today. There have been too many accidents, so now you have to have special permission.

In January 1993, archaeologists in Egypt found the ruins of a small pyramid a few metres from the Great Pyramid of Cheops at Giza. It was discovered by chance during a cleaning operation. This brings the number of known pyramids in the country to 96.

How to build a pyramid . . . (with the help of 80,000 friends)

1   Clear the desert sand to show bare rock.

2   Level the site—perhaps allow water from the Nile to flood the base to give you a level.

3   Use the Pole Star to decide exactly where North is.

4   Make a perfect square for the base and mark the four walls to face north, south, east and west.

5   Starting in the middle, build the first level with limestone blocks of two to three tonnes.

6   Add new levels, each one smaller than the one below. As the levels rise, build ramps of earth to slide the building blocks up.

SHOW OFF!

7   As you build, don't forget to leave passageways and the central burial chamber. That burial chamber must end up directly beneath the point of the pyramid.

8   Cover the finished pyramid with the best Tura limestone and smooth it off.

9   Remove the earth ramps and build a raised stone causeway from the river to the pyramid.

10 Wait for the Pharaoh to die. Mummify him. Bury him in the pyramid with his treasures. And don't forget to seal the pyramid to keep out robbers.

How to decorate a pyramid

1　Find a Pharaoh with a new pyramid—he will need some decorators.

2　Cover the inside walls in a smooth layer of gypsum, or chalk plaster. You will paint on this.

3　Make your brushes by crushing the ends of sticks to give stumpy bristles.

4　Prepare the paints to give nine colours: black, blue, brown, green, grey, red, white and yellow—and the fashionable colour of the New Kingdom, pink.

5　Plan your work carefully by drawing a grid of squares on the walls—then you know where every figure is going to go.

6　Remember the Egyptian style. Heads are painted in profile, that is, sideways, but the eye is shown full face. Legs are more leg-like if they are shown sideways. Shoulders are more shoulder-like if they are both in view. The more important the person, the bigger they are. Pharaoh gets the most space.

Use graph paper to help you copy the drawing above. If you work with some friends you could make a wall painting. DANGER—don't use the living room wall without first asking . . . or you could be history!

The magic of the mummies

Did you know…?

1 Mummy is an Arabic word for "bitumen"—a sort of tar that was precious as a medicine. The Arabs were the first people of modern times to discover mummies and they thought they were covered in bitumen.

2 Egyptians believed that one day the world would end. When it did they would move on to their afterlife. To make that long journey they would need their earthly body. If their body was allowed to rot then they wouldn't be able to go.

3 The men who made dead bodies into mummies were called embalmers. They took the bodies to a place they called the Beautiful House to work on them. The Beautiful House was more like a butcher's shop.

4 At first only the very rich could afford embalming. Later it became a huge industry with even the poorest hoping for it.

48

5 The climate of Egypt is naturally good for preserving a body. A poor peasant died 5,000 years ago and his body was covered by the dry desert sand. It is more perfectly preserved than many mummies and can be seen in the British Museum today. His nickname is Ginger.

6 The human body is made up of 75 per cent water. Anything wet or damp rots very quickly—and dead people in the fierce Egyptian heat were no exception. Something was needed to soak up all the body fluids. At first the embalmers used sand, but this left the skin very tight. Later, the embalmers discovered that natron, a salty chemical found around the sides of lakes near Cairo, did a better job. It left the person looking more like they did when they were alive.

7 Sometimes the embalmers made mistakes and a body was badly mummified. It would turn dark and brittle and bits would break off! If part of a body rotted and fell off—or was snatched by a jackal taking a quick snack when no one was looking- the embalmers replaced it with a wad of linen or a piece of wood. If the person had a limb missing when they were alive the embalmers gave them a wooden one ready for use in the next world.

50

8 Archaeologists have found mummies wrapped in hundreds of metres of linen, up to 20 layers thick.

9 Examination of mummies showed a lot about the bodies when they were alive. Rameses II had a lot of blackheads on his face, while Rameses III had been a very fat man. King Sequenenre II had met a pretty horrible end. There were wounds on his scalp—one wound had pierced his skull. Blood was still clotted in his hair, and his face was twisted in agony. Some think he was murdered in his sleep—others believe he was killed in battle. If so, he may have been mummified quickly, so his hair wasn't cleaned well.

10 In Victorian England people flocked to see a mummy being unwrapped! Doctor Pettigrew at the Royal College of Surgeons provided very popular unwrappings. Even on a bitterly cold January night, tickets were sold out and many important people could not get in. Not even the Archbishop of Canterbury! Refreshments were served after the "performance," just as if it were a theatre show. One of Pettigrew's mummies turned out to be a fake—rags and sticks wrapped up in bandages.

11 The Duke of Hamilton was very impressed by "Mummy" Pettigrew's work. He asked to be mummified by Pettigrew after he died. After twenty years of unwrapping mummies Pettigrew finally had the chance to wrap one. This he did after the Duke died on 18 August 1852. The Duke even had an ancient Egyptian stone coffin waiting for his body. It hasn't been opened since, so we don't know if Pettigrew was as good at making mummies as the Egyptians.

12 When the Egyptians became Christians and later, Muslims, they no longer believed that you needed your earthly body to survive in the afterlife. They didn't need their mummies any more.

Making a mummy

From the evidence we have and the writing of a Greek traveller, Herodotus, this is our best guess at how bodies were mummified.

WARNING: This is very messy! Do not try this in your kitchen! Not even in your school's kitchen!

1   Take a dead Pharaoh.

2   Place the body in a Beautiful House—usually a tent because it keeps the air fresher!

3   Undress the body and put it on a wooden table. This is the embalming table. The table top is not always solid. If the top is just bars of wood you can get underneath the body more easily to put the bandages on later.

4   Remove the brain by placing a chisel up the left nostril and breaking through into the skull.

> *They first take an iron hook and with it draw out the brain through the nostrils.*

(Herodotus—visited Egypt in 455 B.C.)

Sometimes embalmers would go through the head just behind the left eye. They would use a piece of stiff wire with a hook on the end. The wire would be stirred around to cut the brain up into pieces. The pieces would then be scooped out with a different rod with a cup-shaped end.

You can throw the brain away (or feed it to the cat—the Egyptians didn't think the brain was too important in the afterlife.)

5   Fill the empty skull with a packing of natron and plaster—good solid stuff.

53

6   Cut open the front—an embalmer called a "ripper-up" usually does this.

> *They take out the whole contents of the stomach which they then clean, washing it with palm wine. After that they fill the hole with myrrh and other spices. They sew up the opening. The body is placed in natron for 70 days. It is washed and wrapped round from head to foot with bandages of fine linen cloth smeared with gum.*

(The bandages can be as great as 375 square metres—if you're not sure how much that is then cover a basketball court with linen and you'll almost have enough!)

7   If you want, charms and prayers may be written on papyrus (paper) and wrapped in the bandages, or written in ink on the bandages themselves. These will keep away evil spirits—but not grave robbers.

8   You may wish to replace the eyes with polished black stones. (Although when Rameses IV was unwrapped the king had two small onions for eyes!)

9   Stuff the body with linen rags to keep its shape, then sew it up again. Only the heart is left inside. This is very important. It will be weighed later when the king reaches the afterlife.

10   Make a mask for the head. It should look like the person when they were alive. It should also be covered with gold . . . so it's best to make sure the king pays you before he dies!

11   Put the mummy in a coffin (or in a coffin in a coffin in a coffin).

12 Put the stomach, liver, intestines and lungs in their own canopic jars (see page 58), add natron and seal them.

13 Perform the ceremony of opening the mouth of the mummy—if you don't open the mouth then the mummy won't be able to eat, drink, talk or breathe in the afterlife.

14 Fasten down the coffin lid. Place the coffin in a tomb or a pyramid then seal up the tomb. This is to shut out the grave-robbers. (Don't worry about shutting the mummy *in*. The mummy has a Ba—a soul—which can come and go from the tomb as it likes. You'll know a Ba if you ever see one. It has the head of a man and the body of a bird.)

15 Sing a funeral song for the dead. An Egyptian one went like this. . .

> *O gods take this man into your house,*
> *Let him hear just as you hear,*
> *Let him see just as you see,*
> *Let him stand just as you stand,*
> *Let him take his seat just as you take your seat.*

(You'll have to make up your own tune because we don't know how Egyptian music sounded—it was probably a chant with tambourine and drum beats to accompany it.)

16 Have a funeral party with the best wines and food, entertainers and musicians. Everyone's invited—except the mummy!

The fate of the mummy...

The mummy would be placed in its coffin and the coffin placed in the tomb. The dead person would then have to pass through a dangerous place known as the Duat. The dangers were monsters, boiling lakes and rivers of fire. The snake that spat poison was particularly nasty. The monsters could be overcome with the right spells. It was best to write the spells down on Egyptian paper (papyrus) and leave them in or near the coffin. This is the *Book of the Dead*.

If they overcame the monsters then they'd reach the gates of Yaru (the Egyptian afterlife) and meet their friends again. But first they had to pass the greatest test of all in the Hall of Two Truths.

Their heart was weighed. The heart was placed in one side of the balance and in the other side was the Feather of Truth—and the Feather of Truth held all the lies of their past life. The three great gods, Osiris, Anubis and Thoth, decided the result of the weighing.

If the heart passed the test then the dead person was allowed through the gates of Yaru. But if they failed . . . their heart was eaten by a terrifying monster known as the Devourer. This Devourer was part crocodile, part hippopotamus and part lion.

Once the Devourer took your heart . . . you were lost for ever!

Make your own canopic jar...

Intestines can be pretty messy, so it's best to tidy them into a special container. The Egyptians made theirs out of clay. You can make one from a squeeze bottle.

You will need:
- a squeeze bottle
- paints
- modelling clay
- drawing paper
- sand or pebbles
- glue

1   Take the nozzle off the bottle and rinse it out.
2   Wrap a piece of drawing paper round the bottle and cut it to fit.
3   Decorate the paper with hieroglyphics and Egyptian pictures and symbols—look through the book for some ideas.

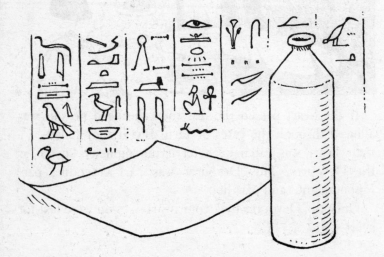

4 Glue the paper to the bottle.

5 Put some sand or pebbles in the bottle to make your canopic jar stand steadily.

6 Use the modelling clay to make a lid. Make the lid into the shape of one of the four Sons of Horus: Imsety—an Egyptian man who guards the liver; Duamutef—a jackal who guards the stomach; Qebehsenuef—a falcon who guards the intestines; Hapi—a baboon who guards the lungs.

QEBEHSENUEF

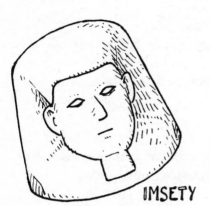

IMSETY

HAPI

DUAMUTEF

59

Some unusual (but true) uses for mummies...

As magic powder
King Charles II of England (1630–1685) used to collect the dust and powder that fell from collections of mummies. He would rub this powder into his skin, all over. He believed that the "ancient greatness" of the mummies would rub onto him.

As fuel
So many mummies were dug up in the 1800s that they became common and worthless. Some were burned as fuel for steam trains when wood and coal were in short supply. Poor people in Thebes used the bandages to heat their ovens.

As ornaments
A display case with the hand or foot of a mummy became a very popular ornament for Victorian mantelpieces.

In witchcraft
William Shakespeare knew about it; "mummy" is an ingredient in the witches' brew in the play *Macbeth*.

In painting
Sixteenth-century artists believed that adding powdered mummy to their paint would stop it cracking when it dried.

A USER'S GUIDE TO MUMMY BITS

As medicine
From the early thirteenth century A.D. till well into the seventeenth century, Egyptian mummies were chopped up and fed to sick people as a cure. It was used for people with all sorts of diseases, as well as broken bones and as a cure for poisoning. So many mummies had left Egypt by the late sixteenth century that the Egyptian government banned their export. Egyptian mummy-sellers then made fake mummies out of any bodies lying around! A French visitor reported seeing 40 fake mummies in a mummy-factory.

In science
The English scientist, Sir Marc Armand Ruffer, thought he could learn about the diseases of ancient Egypt by testing bits of mummies. He found the Egyptians suffered many of the diseases we do today.

In paper-making
Paper made from cloth (rag-paper) has always been valued as high-quality paper. A travelling Egyptian tribe called the Bedouin would steal mummies and sell them to paper-making factories. The American paper manufacturer Augustus Stanwood was still importing mummies at the end of the nineteenth century to turn the bandages into paper. The stained bandages made poor writing paper but was fine for brown paper. It was sold to butchers and grocers as wrapping paper. An outbreak of the deadly disease cholera was traced to the mummy bandages, so the scheme was stopped. Several people died . . . the mummies' revenge?

What would *you* use a mummy for? A shop-window dummy?
A doorstop? A scarecrow? A scare-teacher?

MANNEQUIN   SCARECROW   SCARE TEACHER

EEK

PIT PROP   CHEST OF DRAWERS   TEDDY BEAR

Money from a mummy?

Some very unusual people became involved with the trade in mummies and relics of Egypt. They weren't archaeologists. They were people who saw the chance of making lots of easy money. People like. . .

Giovanni Belzoni

Belzoni was over two metres tall. He used to be part of a fairground strongman act. Then he travelled to Egypt to sell machinery. He soon realized he could make a fortune selling artifacts from the tombs.

His most spectacular exploit was transporting the statue of Rameses II across the desert, down the Nile and over the sea to England. It is now in the British Museum in London.

Before he left Egypt Belzoni was asked, "Are you so short of stones in Europe that you have to come here to take ours?"

"No," he replied. "But we prefer the Egyptian sort."

But even Belzoni wouldn't have dealt with anything as suspect as. . .

Ginger

You probably remember Ginger from page 49. Well, there's this awesome rumour about him. . .

The British Museum was collecting mummies. They already had the well-preserved ones from the tombs. They wanted one from the days before the great Pharaohs and their pyramids. They knew that ordinary Egyptians had been preserved by simple burial in the dry desert sand. Where would they find such a body?

They knew a dealer in Egyptian antiques. He soon found one with reddish-brown hair—it became known as Ginger. And Ginger can still be seen at the British Museum today.

But . . . the Egyptian dealer had a bad reputation for providing forgeries and fakes when he couldn't find the real thing a museum wanted.

Surely he wouldn't "make" a corpse? Surely he wouldn't dry out a freshly killed victim and sell him to the British Museum as a 5,000-year-old mummy?

Surely not.

And anyway, who would he kill?

It seems that about the time that Ginger appeared, the Egyptian dealer's brother disappeared!

Surely he wouldn't . . . would he?

Most gruesome mummy fact. . .
When King Louis XIV of France died in 1715 his heart was mummified as the king had instructed. A nineteenth century Dean of Westminster came into possession of the embalmed heart. He ate it for dinner one evening!

The curse of the mummy's tomb

A true story?

26 November 1922

The great archaeologist Howard Carter had searched for years for a Pharaoh's tomb that hadn't been robbed. The pyramids were empty; the treasures stolen hundreds of years before. But there was still hope that the caves in the Valley of the Kings might have kept their secrets.

At last he arrived at the entrance to an unbroken burial chamber. He called in the organizer of the expedition, Lord Carnarvon, to witness the final breakthrough. Carter described it as follows:

With trembling hands I made a tiny hole in the upper left hand corner. Darkness and empty space, as far as an iron testing-rod could reach, showed that whatever lay beyond was empty. Widening the hole a little, I put in a candle and peered in. At first I could see nothing. The hot air escaping from the chamber caused the candle to flicker a little. But as my eyes became accustomed to the light, details of the room within emerged slowly from the mist; strange animals, statues and gold—everywhere the glint of gold. I was struck dumb with amazement. Lord Carnarvon asked anxiously, "Can you see anything?"

It was all I could do to get out the words, "Yes, wonderful things."

Carter spent years unearthing the most spectacular and precious find this century—he had found the grave of the young king Tutankhamun. But had he released more than hot air from the tomb? Had he also released a 3,000-year-old curse that the ancient Egyptian priests had placed in the tomb to protect the king?

DOOM DOOM DOOM

The curse

The stories erupted quickly. On the day the tomb was opened, the men climbed back into the evening sunshine. As the last one left, a sandstorm sprang up and whirled round the mouth of the cave. When it died away a hawk was seen hovering to the west. The hawk was the symbol of the royal family of Egypt—the west was the direction of the Egyptians' land of the dead.

Lord Carnarvon died on 6 April 1923, less than a year after the discovery. He died from a mosquito bite on his left cheek which became infected. When doctors later examined the mummy of Tutankhamun they noticed a strange mark on the mummy's face . . . on his left cheek!

The night Lord Carnarvon died in the Egyptian capital, Cairo, the city lights failed and plunged the people into darkness. At the same time, back in Hampshire, England, his dog let out a howl and died. "The revenge of Tutankhamun!" people muttered.

In the following months the deaths of several others who had visited the tomb were blamed on the curse. One was an Egyptian prince, Ali Farmy Bey, who could trace his family line back to the Pharaohs. He was murdered in a London hotel and his brother committed suicide.

In 1929 Richard Bethell, who helped Carter to catalogue Tutankhamun's treasures, was thought to have committed suicide. A few months later newspapers reported the death of his father—as the *nineteenth* victim. . .

Today Lord Westbury, aged 78, jumped from the window of his seventh-floor London flat and was instantly killed. Lord Westbury's son, who was formerly the secretary of Howard Carter, the archaeologist at the Tutankhamun diggings, was found last November dead in his apartment, though when he went to bed he appeared to be in the best of health. The exact cause of his death has never been determined. . .

Lord Westbury is supposed to have written: *I can't stand any more horrors* a few days before he died. Police searching the room from which he threw himself found a stone vase. It was a vase from the tomb of Tutankhamun.

The list of deaths grew ever longer. When Archibald Reid, another archaeologist, died as he was about to X-ray a mummy the newspaper headlines screamed: *A shudder is going through England!*

The death of the Egyptologist Arthur Weigall was announced as the *twenty-first* victim of the curse when he died of an "unknown fever." Even the unusual death of an American called Carter was laid at the tombstone of Tutankhamun.

The curse uncovered

Howard Carter called reports of the curse, "ridiculous stories," and claimed they were made up for the amusement of the public.

Howard Carter himself lived until 1939, when he died of natural causes. Surely, as the first man in the tomb, *he* should have been hunted down by any curse? Some of Carter's assistants lived a very long time. Doctor Derry, who examined the body of Tutankhamun, was 88 years old when he died.

In 1933 the German professor Georg Steindorff investigated the curse. He found that neither Lord Westbury, nor his son, had the least connection with the tomb or the mummy. And Richard Bethell probably died of natural causes, not suicide. Steindorff also proved that the American called Carter had no connection at all with Howard Carter.

Mummies were not buried with a "curse," but with a magic spell designed to frighten, not kill, the enemies of the Pharaoh, and to wish the dead king well in the next world.

WARNING
AWESOME SPELLS MAY
SERIOUSLY DAMAGE YOUR HEALTH

The story goes on

However, it's hard to keep a good story down. People love horror films, and walking mummies make ideal monsters. In 1966 the newspapers were off again. That year the Egyptian government decided to lend the Tutankhamun treasures to a Paris museum. An Egyptian museum keeper, Mohammed Ibraham, dreamed that he would face a terrible death if he allowed them to leave the country. He argued against the loan as long as he could. He left the last meeting defeated. The loan would go ahead. As Mohammed left the meeting he was knocked down by a car. He died two days later.

Do you believe in the curse of Tutankhamun?

The mummy's hand

Lots of "true" mummy stories have been told over the past century. This is one of them: see if you believe it!

Lord Carnarvon,
In the name of God, I beg you to take care! The ancient Egyptians had knowledge and power which we people today do not understand!
    Your dear friend,
    Count Louis Hamon

Lord Carnarvon read the letter and snorted with laughter and shook his head, "It'll take more than some crank letter to stop me exploring those tombs!"

Within a few days Lord Carnarvon's expedition found the fabulous tomb of Tutankhamun and four months after that Lord Carnarvon was dead! What had Louis Hamon seen that made him write to warn his friend?

It was his experience with a mummy's hand. . .

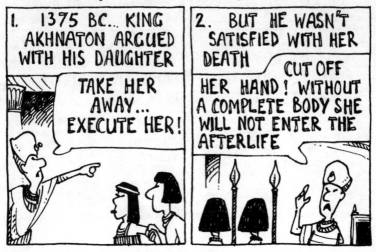

71

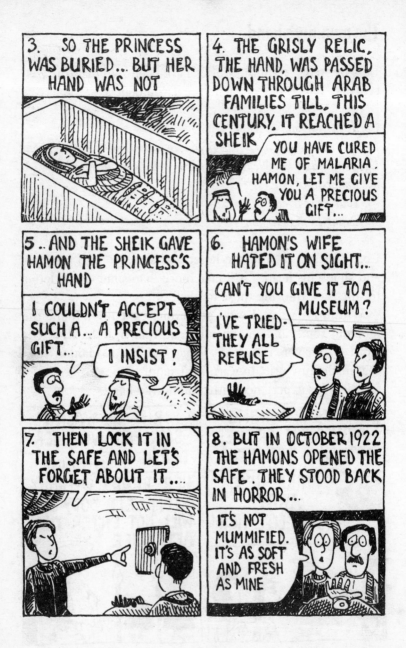

73

Gruesome grave robbers

What power did grave robbers have? They had the power to change the history of Egypt!

Pharaohs built pyramids to keep their mummies safe—grave robbers broke into the pyramids and stole the wealth that was buried with the Pharaohs. So the Pharaohs built bigger and stronger and cleverer pyramids. The grave robbers didn't give in. Every pyramid was robbed.

In the end it was the Pharaohs who gave in. They realized that a pyramid was a huge stone advertisement saying, "Look at my grave! Look at my wealth!" The only answer was to hide the tombs. The Pharaohs switched to being buried in hidden caves in the rocks.

So the Egyptians stopped building pyramids because of the grave robbers. But in the centuries-long battles between grave builders and grave robbers the thieves didn't always have things their own way. . .

The mummy's revenge

The man had reached his goal at last. The stone coffin lay before him. Perhaps it contained untold wealth—enough gold to keep a man for life?

The lid of the coffin was heavy. He struggled to heave it off. The still air of the tomb was disturbed by his struggles. Dust and pebbles fell from the roof. At last a crack appeared in the lid. He paused for a rest, pleased with his work. He set to work with fresh energy. The crack became wider. In his excitement he didn't notice the stones that fell from the limestone roof.

Another heave at the lid. A groaning "Creeeeaak!" echoed through the tomb. He reached a hand into the coffin. Another great "Creeee-aak!" But this time it wasn't the coffin lid. It was the roof of the tomb itself. His struggles to break into the tomb had weakened it. The massive roof slab was slipping down.

Too late he tried to pull his hand free from the coffin. Too late he realized that his own greed was going to kill him. The roof slab fell and crushed him. His grasping hand was still inside the coffin when he died.

And, in 1970, that was how he was found when archaeologists moved the stone to reach the coffin. A skeleton wrapped in a shred of what had once been a coat. A skeleton hand still inside the coffin lid. And in the pocket of the coat was something that shocked them. Something that told them almost exactly when the grave robber had died.

What did they find? The remains of a newspaper. This grave robber had been caught in the coffin in 1944 . . . A.D.!

A grave robber's guide

Cast yourself back in time a few thousand years. You are travelling through ancient Egypt and you've run out of copper coins. You want to rob a pyramid or a rock-tomb (and get away with it). Here are a few hints. . .

1 Remember the penalty for being caught robbing a grave. Torture, then execution. Be careful!

2 Spend a bit of money before you set out. After all you will be fabulously wealthy when you get away with it. Make sure the local officials are on your side. Make friends with them even if it costs you money.

3 Have a gang of seven or eight. Make sure everyone has a useful skill. You may employ. . .

- a couple of expert stonemasons to chisel their way in;
- a smith to melt down your gold and silver;
- a boatman for getting to and from the tombs as well as to act as a lookout;
- water-carriers to keep your masons supplied and to act as labourers.

4 Where possible, find a back way into the tomb. Then it will be a long time before the priests discover the loss. When they check the front entrances the seals will still be in one piece. They will think the mummy is safe—and as long as they think that, then *you* are safe!

5 Bribe everyone concerned with the burial:

The coffin-maker. As he makes the coffin he can turn one end into a trapdoor. That way you won't have to break the seals and raise the lids to get at the mummy. You'll simply open the trapdoor and slide the body out of the end.

The tomb-sealer. He has the job of sealing the

I'M IN A RUT, I SPEND ALL THE MONEY I GET FROM MY LAST TOMB ROBBERY ON BRIBING PEOPLE SO I CAN ROB A TOMB SO I CAN AFFORD TO BRIBE PEOPLE SO I CAN ROB TOMBS

three doors into the tomb. The family will watch him sealing the last door. Pay him well and he will make sure the two inside doors are not sealed. A lot less work for you later on.

The tomb guards. A boring job. A bit of tomb robbing would liven up their lives. Of course you'll have to be sure the tomb is left the way you found it. They can still pretend to guard the tomb even after you have emptied it.

The priests. They are wealthy people. You will have to promise them a lot of money if they are going to "look the other way" when you break in.

The court officials. If word gets around that you have robbed a tomb then the court officials will arrest you. It's best to bribe them first. They can lie for you. They can say, "We have checked and the tomb has never been touched"—and they can protect you from the law.

6 Learn some "tricks of the trade." Here's a quick way to get gold from a tomb: set fire to the tomb! All the wood will turn to ashes—all the gold will melt into pools. When these cool and turn hard they can simply be picked up from the ashes and carted off. Awesome!

7 Make a deal with travelling merchants. They will buy your stolen treasures from you and not ask awkward questions or betray you. (In the twentieth century A.D. these merchants will be known as "fences.")

8 Do not try to spend too much of your treasure at once. Many a tomb robber gave himself away by becoming rich suddenly. People would want to know where the wealth came from.

9 Know the tombs and their passages and rooms well, like a tomb builder—many tomb builders became grave robbers. They grew hungry when their wages were late. They tried going on strike and marching on the officials' houses with chants of "We are hungry! We are hungry!" When that failed they turned to robbing the tombs they'd helped to build.

10 Best of all, try to steal the body before it is buried! Somebody, sometime, did that to the mother of a great Egyptian Pharaoh. Perhaps this is what happened. . .

I've lost my mummy!

Cheops was a vain man, it has to be said. For years the Pharaohs had been buried in pyramids. They were a wonder of his world. But Cheops' had to be the best.

"I want my pyramid to be greater than all the rest. I want the biggest pyramid Egypt has ever seen. I want it to be the biggest the world will ever see."

"Of course, your majesty." Chief Minister Yussef smiled and bowed. "The greatest pyramid for the greatest Pharaoh. I will see to it myself," the man promised. It would make Yussef the most important man in Egypt . . . apart from Cheops, of course. But Yussef could always handle Cheops.

"And I want this pyramid to be safe, Yussef, safe! I want to lie there forever with no grave robbers to destroy my afterlife."

"It will be the safest tomb ever built, your majesty," the Chief Minister promised.

"And the biggest!" Cheops reminded him.

"And the very biggest, your majesty!" Yussef bowed and set about the great task.

Cheops' mother, Hetepheres, sighed. "I'll never live to see it finished, my son."

"Maybe not in this life, but you will watch over it when you reach the afterlife. And one day I will join you there," Cheops promised.

"If the grave robbers allow it, my son."

"The grave robbers shall never enter my Great Pyramid!" Cheops boasted.

Hetepheres coughed gently. "It was my grave I was worried about, my son, not yours."

Cheops rose to his feet. "Mother, I swear by every god that your grave shall be as safe as mine!"

"I hope so," Hetepheres said with a sad shake of the head. "I hope so."

The Great Pyramid of Cheops grew and the years drifted by like the desert sands on the hot Sahara winds . . . and Hetepheres died.

Cheops mourned. The king gave his mother a funeral almost as great as his own was going to be. Thousands lined the dusty roads of Dashur to see Hetepheres' last journey to her resting place. Many thousand eyes saw the jewelled chests, the statues of silver and gold, the figures set in precious stones and the golden furniture follow the old queen to her grave. They watched and they longed for just one tiny part of all that treasure.

But the tomb was sealed with huge stones and guarded night and day. Surely no one could enter . . . someone did.

Yussef brought the terrible news to Cheops. "Impossible!" the king cried. "I promised her! I promised that she'd be safe. Without her body she can never be there to meet me in the afterlife!" Suddenly he turned furiously on his chief minister. "I want everyone responsible killed."

"But the body is safe, your majesty," Yussef said softly. "There is no need for anyone to die."

"Safe?"

"The coffin is still there," Yussef said calmly.

"Thanks to Osiris and Isis!" the king moaned. "But this must never happen again. We must find a second resting place. A secret one . . . somewhere near my own Great Pyramid. The greatest part of all her wealth is still inside that coffin."

"I know, your majesty, I know!" Yussef smiled. "And I have the perfect plan."

Yussef's plan was clever. The grave was so clever and so secret that Hetepheres' grave stayed hidden for 3,000 years. Grave robbers and archaeologists knew about the first tomb and they knew the coffin had been moved. They spent whole lifetimes searching.

They found nothing, until. . .

A photographer was recording the work of some archaeologists near the Great Pyramid of Cheops. He stood the tripod of his camera on the solid rock. One leg of the tripod sank down. Surely nothing sinks through solid rock.

Carefully the archaeologists brushed the sand from the surface. It wasn't rock. It was plaster. It cleverly hid the opening to a shaft. The plaster was cleared but the shaft was filled with blocks of stone. One by one the stones were moved. The shaft was deep. Cut through solid rock, it had been a great feat of mining for Cheops' workers.

Thirty metres down, the archaeologists at last reached the burial chamber. The wooden furniture had crumbled to dust. But the great white stone coffin lay untouched. Just as Cheops had last seen it before the secret burial.

There was only room for eight people in that underground tomb. Only eight were there when the coffin was finally opened. They waited to gaze upon the oldest mummy ever found . . . a mummy buried 2,500 years before the birth of Christ.

But all they found were two silver bracelets—the poor remains from the once fabulous riches of Queen Hetepheres . . . and there was no mummy.

Yet that tomb had never been entered. Poor Cheops had buried an empty coffin. Perhaps he is still wandering through the afterlife looking for his mummy. And perhaps a very crafty Chief Minister is watching him . . . and still smiling.

The grave robbers of modern times

The priests of ancient Egypt slipped silently through the moonless darkness. Their servants carried the awesome burden—30 mummies! But the priests weren't grave robbers, they were grave rescuers.

Robbers had been coming to the Valley of the Kings and stripping the graves of their riches. Not satisfied with just taking the gold, they had been tearing open the mummies' bandages to get at the hidden jewels. Everyone knew who was doing the thieving. No one could stop them. The robbers had friends in high places. When they were caught they were released time after time.

The loyal and caring priests could do just one last act to save their god-kings and queens. Move them. So in a secret operation, the mummies of some of the greatest kings were taken from the broken tombs and placed together in a new and hidden home, deep beneath the rocky valley.

The tattered bandages were patched, the bodies had new labels placed on them and the few treasures that were left were put with them. Then the tomb was sealed and the entrance disguised. That should keep thieves out. And it did for thousands of years.

Historians knew about the 30 great kings and queens— but archaeologists couldn't tell them where they had been buried. Then, in the 1880s, a new gang of grave robbers solved the mystery. . .

Mohammed's story

Mohammed was fed up. His feet were almost too tender to walk on. His body was a mass of bruises. He hobbled along the street to his brother's house and almost collapsed. His oldest brother, Ahmed, led him to a chair and brought him strong coffee. "Did you tell them anything?" Ahmed asked.

Mohammed glared at him fiercely, proudly. "The police tied me up. They threw me to the floor of a cell. They beat me on the soles of my feet till I thought they were on fire!"

"But did you tell them anything?" another brother demanded.

"Not a thing!" Mohammed hissed. "They wanted to know where we got our money from. I told them we worked for it. So they beat me. They asked me what I knew about ornaments stolen from the tombs . . . I said I knew nothing. So they beat me again."

"You were brave, Mohammed," a younger brother smiled.

"I saved your miserable skins," Mohammed sneered.

"We are grateful," Abdul nodded.

Mohammed leaned forward. "How grateful?"

"Very grateful!"

"I mean how much money is my silence worth?" Mohammed went on as he sipped at the strong, black coffee.

The brothers shrugged. "We have always shared the money. Everything is split equally between the five of us."

"I want half in future," Mohammed said.

The brothers looked at one another. One gave a small laugh. Another joined in. Soon Mohammed's four brothers were roaring with laughter. Ahmed recovered enough to say, "You forget that I found the tomb of 30 mummies back in 1871. If anyone deserves half it is me!"

"And if you hadn't been so greedy, selling too many things, those museum people would never have put the police on to us," Mohammed argued. "I want more! I have suffered for it."

Ahmed rose to his feet, the laughter gone. "No!"

Mohammed threw the coffee cup to the floor and stumbled to the door. "So be it," he muttered as he limped into the night. Within minutes Mohammed was tapping on the door of the museum official's house.

"Mr. Maspero?" he asked.

"He is away. I am his assistant, Emil Brugsch. Can I help you?"

"No. But I can help you," Mohammed said, and he told his story. Brugsch listened in silence as Mohammed explained how Ahmed had found the tomb. He had been looking for a lost goat when he came across the entrance to a steeply sloping tunnel. When he returned with a lantern he found a burial chamber with 30 mummies and their treasures.

Of course, any treasures found belonged to the Museum of Egypt. It was against the law to sell them. But he told his brothers about the find. For more than ten years they had been selling the treasures, a few at a time, secretly to collectors.

"And will you lead me to this burial chamber?" Brugsch asked.

Mohammed nodded. "The last time we were in trouble Mr. Pawar, the mayor of Western Thebes, spoke up for us . . . we paid him well, of course. Will you make sure I do not go to prison, Mr. Brugsch?"

Brugsch laughed. "If all you tell me is true, Mohammed, then you will not go to prison . . . you will become a hero of the Egyptian nation!"

"The stolen treasures. . ."

"Oh, they don't matter too much. It's the mummies we want to get our hands on. Shall we go?"

Brugsch found the tombs but had to fight to save his precious mummies. Men from a nearby town heard about the find and wanted to stop the archaeologist taking their dead kings from them. As they headed down the Nile to the Museum at Cairo, the local people lined the banks and wailed and ground dust into their heads, just as the ancient Egyptians did thousands of years before.

Then, on the journey, thieves attacked the boat and tried to take its treasures. This time they were too well guarded. At last they reached the safety of the Cairo Museum. And what do you think happened to Mohammed? Was he. . .

A   Sent to prison?
B   Given a £500 reward?
C   Executed?
D   Given a job in charge of the burial excavations?
E   Killed by a curse on the mummy's tomb?

Answer: **B** and **D**.

The remarkable river

What has the Nile River got to do with the pyramids?

Everything. No Nile River . . . no pyramids.

North Africa used to be rich grassland. The part that is now Egypt was all flooded. Then, about 9,000 years ago, the region began to dry out and people moved in. It became drier still, so the people moved to the strip of land near the river—the Nile. But why did they start to build?

Here are four clues. Can you see how each clue might lead to making pyramids?

1   Every year the Nile flooded and gave the farmers enough rich soil for their crops. But of course they couldn't work the land when it was flooded.

2   The area outside the Nile's flood valley became desert—difficult for other people to cross. Egypt was a land cut off from the rest of the world. No troublesome neighbours.

3   The farmers had no wheeled transport. But in the floods, when their houses and villages were cut off, they learned to build boats.

4   The rains fell in the tropical forests of Africa and rushed down the Nile to make it flood. The people of Egypt never really saw much rain; the sudden, life-giving Nile floods seemed to be a magical gift.

Here are the four sides of a pyramid that might explain the link between the Nile and the pyramids.

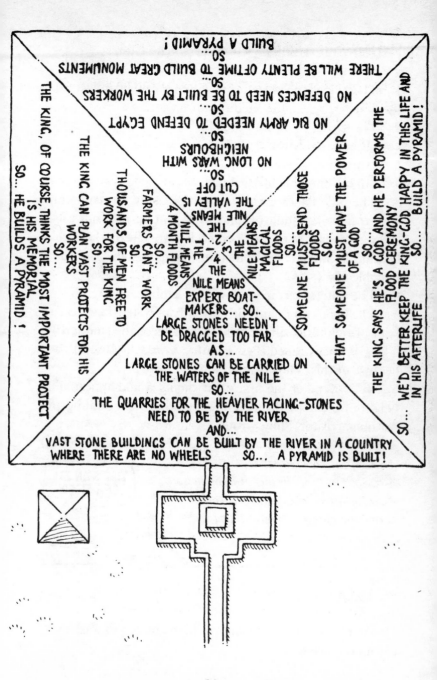

Flatten your friends with facts on the Nile...

1   The Nile is an awesome 960 kilometres (600 miles) from the first cataract to the Mediterranean sea.

2   Three rivers flow into the Nile:
   • the Atarba River of Sudan
   • the Blue Nile of Ethiopia
   • the White Nile of Uganda.

3   The Nile floods arrive at almost exactly the same time each year—the middle of June. Marks on the riverside rocks showed the height of the flood each year. The marked rocks became known as "Nileometers"—an awesome fact, or a horrible fib?

4   The waters start to go down in October.

5   The floods don't only bring plenty of water. They leave a layer of rich black silt, or mud, which keeps the land fertile. The Egyptians called their country *Keme*, the Black Land, because of this. They planted lots of crops.

6   By November the first plant shoots would appear. The height of the flood decided how well the crops would grow. A Roman visitor, Pliny, wrote:

A rise of twelve ells meant hunger. (An ell was about 1.5 metres)
A rise of thirteen ells meant suffering.
A rise of fourteen ells meant happiness.
A rise of fifteen ells meant security.
A rise of eighteen ells meant disaster.

THIS IS AN ELL OF A FLOOD

Disaster was when the flood was high enough to wash away the mud houses!

7   Herodotus, a Greek visitor, wrote:
> *When the Nile overflows the land*
> *is converted into a vast sea, and*
> *nothing appears but the cities, which*
> *look like islands.*

8   The Nile was the main road through Egypt. Most long journeys were made by boat.

9   The Nile no longer floods. A vast dam (opened at Aswan in 1971) now controls the flow. But the dam has brought unexpected problems. No floods—no silt. The soil becomes tired and farmers now have to pay for chemical fertilizers to replace the nutrients that the Nile brought for free every year.

10   The Nile has poems and songs written about it. A priest wrote this one:
> *Hail to you, O Nile. . .*
> *You have come to feed Egypt. . .*
> *When you flood the land rejoices. . .*
> *Joy when you come, O Nile!*
> *Joy when you come!*
> *You who feed men and animals. . .*
> *Joy when you come!*

(It might not be a great pop song—but it's lasted over 3,000 years.)

11 The desert began where the floodwater ended. The difference was so clear that a person could stand with one foot in a field and the other in barren sand. The desert was known as *Dashre*, the Red Land.

POOR DEVIL, HE NEARLY MADE IT

12 The Egyptian year was divided into three seasons based on the Nile: flood season, planting season and harvesting season.

13 The peasants had to build and repair irrigation channels each year. This was part of the tax they paid to the Pharaoh. The punishment for trying to miss working on the Pharaoh's projects was a beating. It was no use trying to run away because if you weren't caught then your family would be punished instead.

14 Floodwater could be "trapped" in reservoirs when the river sank. The fields would then have a water supply even when the river wasn't flooded. To lift the water into the fields the farmers used a *shaduf*. This was a trellis holding up a pole, with a counterweight on one end. On the other end was a bucket that could be lowered into the water. This invention meant that one man could lift thousands of gallons of water in a day. It was so easy to make and so successful that shadufs are still used today. You can try modelling one yourself.

Shock your friends with a shaduf

Egyptian peasants can make a shaduf out of tree branches; you can make yours look real by making one out of twigs.

1 Collect three straight twigs about twenty centimetres (or eight inches) long. Tie them together, but not too tightly, about three centimetres (one inch) from one end. Leave some spare string hanging loose at the knot.

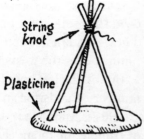

2 Stand the twigs up and spread the other ends out so they make a frame or trellis (see picture at right.) Push the ends into Plasticine to hold the frame steady.

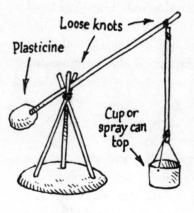

3 Find another straight twig, about 35 centimetres (fourteen inches). This will be the lever. Using the slack string, tie this to the top of the frame, where the other twigs meet. Tie the lever about twelve centimetres (five inches) from one end (see left.)

4 Weight the shorter part of the lever with Plasticine. Tie another twig, about fifteen centimetres (six inches) to the long end of the lever.

5 Now you need something for a bucket—the bottom of a plastic cup or the top of a spray can would do. Make three holes in this and tie it to the twig hanging from the lever.

Congratulations—you have just made a simple but awesome invention!

93

A gallery of gods

What a life—spending half your time worrying about death! And death was an awesome problem for the Egyptians. They wanted to reach the spirit world that the priests taught about.

This wasn't as good as "the land of the gods" that the dead Pharaohs went to, but it was better than life on Earth. They even knew where their spirit world was in the sky . . . juuuust over the western horizon.

But by the left kneecap of Anubis! There was an awesome number of gods for an Egyptian to please before he or she got there. And if they annoyed one, well, it was shadufs-full of trouble for them. (Erm . . . sorry Anubis, I think you've got a very nice kneecap.)

You see, the gods were unbelievably old. They had lived before people existed and now treated humans as if they were a mixture of toys and servants. The gods controlled the world and everything that happened. They demanded respect.

Try keeping this lot happy:

Sobek—the crocodile-headed god. He controlled water supplies.

Thoth—the ibis-headed god of wisdom who invented speaking and writing.

Set—god of the desert and storms. The enemy of Osiris.

94

Re—the Sun God. Some said he had made people. The Egyptians called themselves, "the cattle of Re."

Horus—the falcon-headed god who looked after the Pharaoh.

Sekhmet—the lioness goddess of war.

Hathor—the cow-horned goddess of love. She also looked after happiness, dancing and music.

Ptah—the god who spoke the names of all the things in the world. By doing this he made them exist. (Neat trick, eh? If only I could do that . . . ice cream, Mars bar, trip to Disney World. . .)

Isis—wife of Osiris. She took special care of women and children.

Bes—the dwarf god of happiness, and protector of the family.

Anubis—the jackal-headed god of the dead. He helped to prepare mummies.

Osiris—god of death and rebirth, the Underworld and the Earth. Long ago he had taught people to farm.

Awesome answers to powerful problems

Which god would you pray to? Fill in the missing name.

O great .... My land is short of water and my crops are dying.

Mighty .... My youngest son died of fever three months ago. Since then my wife is heartbroken. Please help her to enjoy life again.

O wise .... My son wishes to be a scribe, but is so bad at learning his hieroglyphs that his teachers are threatening to throw him out of school. Beatings don't seem to help.

Please give me strength, O vengeful .... Raiders from the Red Land have attacked our village. Help us to defeat them.

O powerful .... My husband has died and I have spent most of my savings on his mummification to please you. Please help him to reach the spirit world.

Please, sweet .... I am madly in love with the most beautiful girl, but she laughs at my dancing. I am terribly clumsy and fall over my own feet.

ERRRRR

GO ON! DO YOU WANT TO DANCE WITH HER OR DON'T YOU!

Pray like an Egyptian

The story that all Egyptians believed was this one. . .
Osiris was an awesome king, everyone agreed . . . or almost everyone. He was loved by his loyal wife, Isis, and all of his people . . . well, almost all. Only Osiris's brother, Set, hated him. He was jealous. So Set plotted and Set planned. How could he kill his brother and get away with it?

What if the body of Osiris was never found? Yes, that was it! Make sure the body was never found.

It was a gruesome job, but Set had to do it. First he killed Osiris . . . and then he cut the body up into fourteen parts. He scattered the pieces along the banks of the Nile and left the crocodiles to finish off the job.

But the plan failed. Isis travelled far and wide to find the fourteen parts of her husband's body, and she carefully put them back together. She then wrapped Osiris's body in linen bandages to hold him in one piece. Osiris had become Egypt's first mummy.

Isis still wasn't finished. She now called on the god Anubis for help. Anubis breathed life back into Osiris. Osiris couldn't come back to Earth as a man; instead he went to the afterlife as the god of the dead.

Anubis became the god of preserving the body for the afterlife. Isis became the goddess who protects the dead. And Set? Set had to deal with Horus, the son of Osiris and Isis. Set managed to pluck out Horus's eye in their long and grisly battle. But in the end, Horus won. Set was doomed to spend the rest of time in the gruesome Underworld of the evil dead.

Horus went on to become the protector of the living . . . while his plucked eye became a way of allowing the dead to see.

I SPY WITH MY LITTLE EYE...

Charm your friends

The Egyptians believed such stories and were very superstitious. They also believed in lucky charms. Here is one you could make for yourself out of card to wear around your neck.

The three symbols are Egyptian hieroglyphic signs for three words. . .

⛩ "all"   ☥ "life"   ♀ "protection."

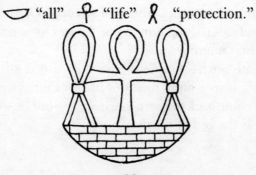

Awesomely troublesome Egyptians

O Pharaoh it isn't fair-o

They get the best food that there is on Earth,
They're treated like gods from the day of their birth . . . the Pharaohs.

They live in a palace all graceful and tall,
While their servants slave on they do no work at all . . . the Pharaohs.

Their graves are those pyramids up to the sky,
They have a fine afterlife, they never die . . . the Pharaohs.

But who builds the pyramids? Who sweats and slaves?
Who works . . . then ends in a dusty old grave? . . . the peasants!

The horriblest thing to be in Egyptian history was a peasant in the Old Kingdom. They were at the bottom of a pyramid that looked like this.

1   The Pharaoh—king, chief priest and god, commander of the armies.

2   The vizier—the second most powerful man. He had to see that the country was running smoothly: everything from collecting taxes to organizing the building of irrigation systems. He was also chief judge.

3   The *imakhu* (the honoured ones)—friends and family of the Pharaoh. They got all the best jobs: jobs like . . . General Ambassador, Governor of a district, Keeper of the Crown Jewels, Keeper of the Oils and Perfumes, Keeper of the King's clothes . . . or, Keeper of the Secret of all the Royal Sayings—that means being in control of who gets to talk to the Pharaoh.

4   The *nomarchs*—local barons who control small districts. They are directly in charge of most of the people, they keep order and raise armies if Egypt is attacked.

5   The scribes—educated officials who keep the written records.

6   The priests—thousands who run the temples to the many gods.

7   The *hemutiu* or craftsmen—skilled workers who look after the needs of the wealthy—weavers, architects, painters, sculptors, traders, jewellers, embalmers, metal workers. . .

8   The peasants—the remaining 90 per cent.

101

How to be a peasant in ten hard lessons

1   There are few slaves in Egypt—but a peasant has to work so hard he may as well be one.
2   Peasants are like property—if a Pharaoh gives land to a nobleman then the peasants are thrown in with it.
3   Peasants are counted along with the cattle to show how rich a landowner is.
4   Women aren't counted because they are not worth as much as cattle!

BUT IF YOU CUT MY FINGER OFF I'LL DO EVEN LESS WORK

5 Peasants are organized into work gangs of about five.

6 Families may be broken up to work in different gangs.

7 When a peasant can't work on his land because the Nile is in flood he is ordered to work on the pyramids.

8 If a peasant doesn't work hard enough then he will be punished by whipping or by having bits chopped off his body—a finger or a toe, perhaps.

9 If you try to get really rich with a bit of tomb robbing then the bit they chop off will be your head!

Before crops are harvested the Pharaoh's taxman will come around to work out the Pharaoh's share. The good news is that the peasant's family can have what the Pharaoh leaves!

Working in the fields

NOW.. YOU HORRIBLE PEASANT, THE FLOODS HAVE GONE DOWN. HERE'S A LITTLE LIST OF JOBS TO KEEP YOU BUSY.

1. REPAIR DAMAGE TO THE FIELDS CAUSED BY THE FLOODS
2. BREAK UP THE SOIL WITH HOES AND PLOUGH IT BEFORE THE SUN BAKES IT TOO HARD
3. SOW THE SEEDS AND USE ANIMALS (LIKE A HERD OF GOATS) TO TREAD THEM IN
4. KEEP THE FIELDS WATERED AS THE CROPS GROW
5. KEEP THE FIELDS WEEDED
6. SCARE THE BIRDS AWAY
7. HARVEST THE EARS OF WHEAT OFF THE TOP OF THE STALKS
8. THRESH THE CORN – BEAT IT WITH FLAILS TO SEPARATE THE GRAIN FROM THE HARD CHAFF ON THE OUTSIDE
9. WINNOW THE CORN – TOSS THE GRAIN IN THE AIR SO THE LIGHT CHAFF IS BLOWN AWAY
10. GO BACK TO CUT THE CORN STALKS FOR ANIMAL FEED, FOR MAKING BRICKS AND FOR BASKET MAKING

WHAT DO I DO IN MY SPARE TIME?

I'M GLAD YOU ASKED ME THAT ... YOU CAN LOOK AFTER THE PIGS AND SHEEP AND GEESE AND DUCKS – AND THEN GROW SOME GRAPES FOR WINE THEN GROW SOME FLAX TO MAKE LINEN, THEN GRIND THE CORN ....

I WISH I HADN'T ASKED. I'LL BE GLAD WHEN THE FLOOD SEASON RETURNS AND I CAN GET BACK TO WORK ON THE PYRAMIDS!

Working on the pyramids

You have dragged a huge, stone block for 60 kilometres over the burning desert. The only water you have is what you can carry with you. At last you reach the pyramid, haul the stone into place and stagger off for your pay of bread and linen and ointment. That's when the leader of the work gang gives you the dreadful news . . . no pay!

You trudge back to your barracks—rough limestone shelters with mud floors. You are tired, hungry and angry. The rooms are crowded and there's no proper water supply or toilet. The place stinks from human sewage and from the animals you share your lodgings with.

You wish you were back home with your wife and children. But you know you will die of starvation before you get there.

What will you do? You could. . .
1 Grumble and go back to work.
2 Send a begging letter to the Pharaoh.
3 Go on strike.

THESE CONDITIONS ARE NOT FIT FOR A PEASANT

Answer: 3. The first recorded strike in the history of the world was held on the site of a pyramid. The workers sat in the shade and refused to go back to work until they had been paid their rations. They were paid!

Ancient Egyptian ancient joke

It's no wonder there was trouble in the Old Kingdom. Around 2300 B.C. the Old Kingdom began to fall apart. The power of the Pharaohs was challenged by the nomarchs. An old text explained:

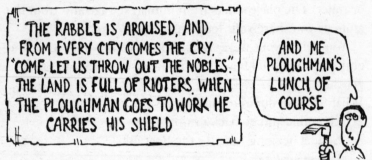

It wasn't until 2065 B.C. (and the Pharaohs of the eleventh dynasty) that control was restored again. The peasants were offered better conditions.

They were allowed to organise themselves into family groups. Each family was given enough land to feed itself. The fields were passed down from generation to generation and could not be taken away. The peasants were happier.

Wonderful women

How to be a wonderful Egyptian woman

The Egyptians had a clear idea of what made a wonderful Egyptian woman . . . the goddess Isis. To be a wonderful woman all you had to do was be like Isis, who. . .

How to be a fairly wonderful Egyptian woman

If being like Isis was too difficult then you could be a fairly wonderful woman by. . .

1 Staying at home and obeying your parents until you were twelve years old and old enough to marry;

2 Marrying someone suitable— someone mum and dad approved of;

3 Obeying your husband;

4 Sharing your husband with several other wives;

5 Giving your husband lots of children—six or seven were not unusual.

How to be a normal Egyptian woman

Not many Egyptian women managed to be quite so perfect. In fact. . .

1 Girls with richer parents would leave home and go to school and learn to read or write.

2 Girls often married for love rather than have their parents choose a husband. It was common to marry someone in the family, such as an uncle or a cousin.

3 A Greek visitor, Herodotus, wrote that Egyptian women were not as obedient as he felt they should be. He complained they were much too independent!

4 An Egyptian man could have as many wives as he liked but he had to be able to keep them all in comfort. The chief wife was the equal of her husband and her first son would get his wealth when he died—the chief wife would get his household goods.

CHIEF WIFE
ASSISTANT CHIEF WIFE
WIFE #1
WIFE #2
TRAINEE WIFE

5 Girls often had their first baby when they were just twelve or thirteen years old. Women gave birth kneeling on special bricks. Childbirth was a dangerous time because of the high risk of infection. It was common for mother or baby to die. A woman had to hope that the goddess of childbirth, Twaret, would keep away evil spirits. Twaret should have been able to manage that—she was a ferocious, pregnant hippopotamus!

How to be a beautiful Egyptian woman

Egyptian women were proud of their appearance and loved to be fashionable. If the Egyptians had a book of beauty tips they might have told you. . .

1 Bathe often. Purify the water with natron—yes, the salt used to preserve mummies!

2 Have a massage. A servant will give you a massage—if you're lucky enough to have a servant.

3 Use eye makeup. Take the lead-ore, galena, to make a grey-black mascara and use it to give an almond shape to the eye. Pluck your eyebrows. Silver tweezers are best—if you can afford them, of course.

4 Use face makeup. Brighten your face with blush and lipstick made out of red iron-oxides.

5 Use nail-colour. Mix up some henna to give a red tint to the nails—and it can also be used to colour the palms of your hands and the soles of your feet!

110

Live like an Egyptian

The Egyptians lived in houses built of mud bricks. That's not at all horrible. The mud was free and the bricks, baked by the hot summer sun, became rock hard. Mud houses could last for hundreds of years and some Egyptians still build their homes with mud today. The more important you were, the bigger your house. Egyptians had very little furniture, but that didn't matter because they spent so much time outdoors. Would you like to have lived like an Egyptian?

WELL I SUPPOSE BUILDING MUD-BRICK HOUSES NAKED CUTS DOWN ON LAUNDRY BILLS

1 Egyptians wore very few clothes. Children and poor people often wore nothing. But luckily the ancient Egyptians lived in a very warm, dry country . . . and walking around with no clothes was an obvious thing to do.

2 Egyptians ate bread. It was so rough that it wore away their teeth! There were bakeries in Egypt in 2000 B.C. If you want an idea of how the bread would taste (without wearing out your teeth) try this recipe. . .

111

Wholemeal bread....

You need:
1. 4 cups of wholemeal flour.
2. half a teaspoon of salt.
3. 2 cups of warm water.

Method:
1. Mix the flour, salt and water
2. Knead well for five minutes
3. Shape the dough into circles or triangles
4. Place the shapes on a greased baking tray.
5. Leave overnight.
6. Decorate the edges of the shapes with finger-dents.
7. Bake in an oven at 350°F for half an hour.

(You can add a cup of chopped dates – shapes could be Egyptian animals if you like)

Your Verdict (Tick the box): Awesome ☐   Okay ☐
Horrible ☐

3   Egyptian food included cucumbers, celery, lettuce, onions, garlic, leeks and cress . . . but most people had to live on bread and onions. Their fruits were melons, figs, pomegranates and dates. Grapes were used for wine, and honey for sweetening. The later Egyptians grew cherries, apples and pears. Sheep, goats, cattle and geese gave them meat, but pigs were thought unclean.

4   They drank a type of beer made from barley. Bread was added to barley and water, and left to brew. The liquid had to be strained before it could be drunk, and it probably looked more like soup!

5 The Egyptians made the world's first known sweets as early as 1600 B.C. The recipes were found inscribed on stone tablets. Try this one. . .

Date sweetmeats....

You need:
1. 1 cup of dates
2. 1 teaspoon of cinnamon spice
3. half a teaspoon of cardamom seeds
4. half a cup of chopped walnuts
5. a little warm honey
6. a saucer of ground almonds.

Method:
1. Stir the dates with a little water to make a paste (using a blender is quicker but not so original).
2. Stir in the cinnamon and cardamom.
3. Using your (clean!) hands mix in the chopped walnuts.
4. Shape the date-and-walnut mix into sweet-sized spheres.
5. Brush the sweets with honey.
6. Dip them in ground almond powder.
7. Eat them!

6 The Egyptians trained Ethiopian baboons to pick their dates from the trees. (If you happen to have a date tree in your back garden maybe you could train your parents to be your baboons?)

7   The Egyptians were great believers in magic. Here is the most useful hint you will ever find in a book! It might well save your life! If you are unlucky enough to fall into a river full of crocodiles, say,

HAIL YOU MONKEY SEVEN CUBITS TALL WHOSE EYES ARE MADE OF GOLD AND WHOSE LIPS ARE FIRE AND WHOSE WORDS ARE LIKE FLAMES... HOLD THE CROCODILE SO THAT I CAN GET UP SAFELY!

SCRATCH SCRATCH

Say it quickly and say it in Egyptian. It is guaranteed to work . . . if it doesn't then you can have your money back.

8   Egyptians cropped their hair short because of the heat. But rich Egyptians wore wigs on important occasions. Then, on top of the wig they might wear a white cone of wax. The wax was mixed with perfume. As the event wore on, the wax melted, the perfume was released . . . and the wax ran all over your wig!

9 Egyptian medicine was a mixture of common sense and magic. A government official, Khety, was attacked and received a serious head wound. His doctor was able to drug Khety to sleep then remove part of his damaged skull; the wound was sewn up—and Khety lived.

10 On the other hand, a cure for blindness involved mashing up the eye of a pig with honey and red ochre and pouring it in the patient's ear!

If you have a stomach ache you can try reciting this ancient Egyptian charm as you drink your medicine, "Come, you who drive out evil things from my stomach and my limbs. He who drinks this shall be cured just as the gods above were cured."

What was it for?

Take a look at these awesome Egyptian objects, and see if you can work out how the Egyptians would have used them.

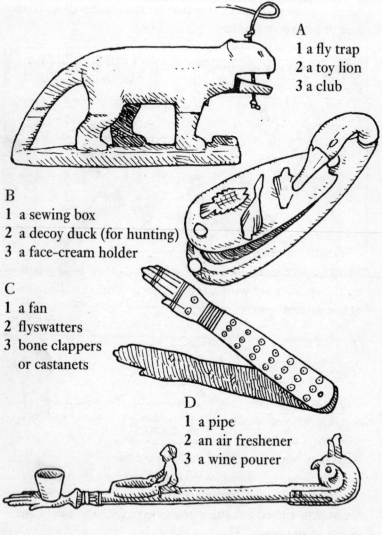

A
1 a fly trap
2 a toy lion
3 a club

B
1 a sewing box
2 a decoy duck (for hunting)
3 a face-cream holder

C
1 a fan
2 flyswatters
3 bone clappers or castanets

D
1 a pipe
2 an air freshener
3 a wine pourer

Answers: A.2 B.3 C.1 D.2.

Awesome Egyptian entertainment

Storytelling

The ancient Egyptians were fond of stories. This one is a bit like our own fairy tales:

When Prince Ramesside was born, the Goddess of Fate visited his cradle. "This child will be killed by a crocodile, a snake or a dog," she said.

The king, his father, protected the boy well, but when he grew he left home and learned of a beautiful princess in Syria. The man who could climb her tower would win her hand in marriage.

Of course Prince Ramesside won and married the princess.

His life seemed happy . . . until he was attacked by a snake! The princess saved him that time.

His life seemed happy . . . until he was attacked by his own dog. He ran into the sea and saved himself!

He seemed safe . . . till a crocodile swam up to him. A very hungry crocodile! The crocodile gave the prince just one chance. Prince Ramesside could go free if he'd agree to kill one of the crocodile's greatest enemies. . .

Unfortunately, the ancient papyrus paper is damaged and we've lost the end of the story. Sorry! Perhaps you'd like to think of an ending. Here's a clue—the Egyptians liked a sad story with a happy ending!

Children's games

A ball would be made from leather and stuffed with grain. Catching and juggling were popular. Sometimes the catchers would ride "piggyback" while they threw or juggled.

Spinning-tops of polished stone were made for children—they would be spun with the fingers. The trick was to keep more than one going at a time.

Knee races could be run. All you have to do is race between two points . . . but your hands must never leave your knees!

Beautifully made toys have been found in tombs. Wooden animals had mouths that would open and close when you tugged the string.

Goat-on-the-ground game

Try playing this simple Egyptian game. You need a group of four or more.

1 Two players are the "Goat."

2 The two players who are the Goat sit on the ground, face to face with legs outstretched.

3 The others have to jump over the Goat without being caught by the Goat's hands.

4 If a jumper is caught then the jumper becomes half of the Goat.

MY, THAT WAS A HIGH JUMP

Water sport

Okay, check your swimming certificates. You need two teams of three or four people with a boat for each team. The aim is to stand in your boats and knock the other team into the water, one by one, without being knocked in yourself. You could try it on grass with two teams standing on planks!

Hunting

Hunt the hippopotamus with harpoons, spears, ropes and nets—highly dangerous—the hippo might decide to hunt the hunter!

Do not try this sport! (You may find a hippo in your local zoo but you'll be thrown out if you try to kill it . . . and even if you succeeded you'd never get it in the microwave.)

Hunting birds—the Egyptians would use tame birds to attract the wild ones, then kill the wild birds with a "throwing stick"—a sort of boomerang that doesn't come back.

Try hitting cardboard cut-out birds with "throwing sticks"—the most hits out of ten throws, wins.

Alquerque

This Spanish game is thought to have come originally from ancient Egypt. It was probably introduced into Spain by the Moors—who lived in North West Africa. The Moors had conquered Egypt in the Middle Ages. You will need twelve counters each and a game board. You can draw out a game board like the one below on a piece of cardboard. Only two people can play. Set the pieces out as shown below.

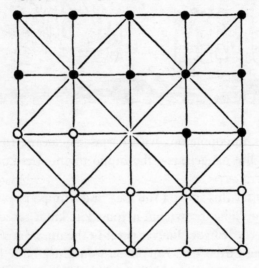

Rules:

1 Only the space in the middle is left clear.

2 Throw a die to decide who goes first and the first move has to be into the middle.

3 Then into any empty place, but pieces can only be moved along the lines of the board.

4 You can capture a piece and take it off the board as you would in checkers, by jumping over it. You can capture more than one piece in the same move.

5 The winner is the player who captures all the opponent's pieces.

Awesome astronomy

Marking time
The Egyptian calendar was awesomely brilliant. Some historians think it was their greatest invention. By observing the sun they calculated the length of the year at 365 days, almost the same as ours.

The year was divided into the three seasons you read about on page 92, each 120 days long with five "extra" days each year. There were twelve months of 30 days each. There were three weeks in a month. There were ten days in a week.

Ancient records

Some time around 3000 B.C. an astronomer was observing the sky just before dawn. He was working in the academy at Memphis, the new capital city of united Upper and Lower Egypt. It was the first day of the Inundation, or flood season.

On the eastern horizon the sun began to rise—but on this day at the same time, so did the star Sothis (we call it the Dog Star, or Sirius.) For generations afterwards they kept watch and discovered that these three events—the start of the flood season, the rising of the sun and the rising of Sothis happened . . . wait for it . . . once every 1,460 years. Awesome!

If we count the working life of an astronomer as about 25 years, think about how many generations searched the sky—don't be lazy, work it out—25 into 1,460—mumble . . . mumble . . . mumble . . . okay, okay, you can turn the page upside down to find out.

Answer: 58 generations and someone doing a ten-year shift.

Write like an Egyptian no. 1

The Egyptian writing is called hieroglyphics . . . but the Egyptians didn't call it that! The word is Greek from *heiros* meaning sacred and *gluphe* meaning carving. The Egyptian name for it meant "words of the gods."

Sometimes a hieroglyphic sign meant a letter—the way it does with our alphabet. Sometimes it meant a whole word.

The "ink" was more like our poster paints. The most common colours were red and black. The ink would be made with gum into blocks of colour, not liquid ink. (That would dry up too quickly in the Egyptian climate.)

The "pen" would be more like a fine brush. A twig or reed would be chewed till the end was frayed like the bristles of a brush. It would then be trimmed with a knife to a very fine tip. The pen was dipped in water and then rubbed on the ink-block.

The "paper" was called papyrus. The soft insides of reeds were taken out and laid in a criss-cross pattern. They were then hammered together to a smooth surface and dried in the sun. The longest known papyrus is an awesome 125 metres long.

Hieroglyphs were deliberately complicated so that it took a long time to read and write them. It meant that those who could read and write were more important.

Most Egyptian boys who went to school were sent there to become scribes. They had to learn to read and write before they could train for good jobs such as a civil servant, doctor or priest. Most Egyptian children stayed at home and were trained to do the same jobs as their parents.

Schools were often in temples and run by priests. Learning to be a scribe was hard. Discipline was strict and the teachers awesomely stern. Just read this text that has survived, called *Advice to a Young Scribe*. . .

O SCRIBE DO NOT BE IDLE, OR YOU SHALL BE CURSED. DO NOT GIVE YOUR HEART TO PLEASURE OR YOU SHALL FAIL. DO NOT SPEND A DAY IN IDLENESS OR YOU SHALL BE BEATEN. A BOY'S EAR IS ON HIS BACKSIDE AND HE LISTENS WHEN HE IS BEATEN...

HELP!

When the last temple was closed in the sixth century A.D., the skill of reading hieroglyphs was lost. This is why people thought that the ancient Egyptians were so brilliant that they had invented a language no one else was clever enough to understand.

In 1799 the Rosetta Stone was discovered by an officer in Napoleon's army. This had the same message carved into it in both hieroglyphs and Greek lettering. In 1822 a young French scholar, Jean-Francois Champillon, used the stone and his knowledge of Greek to crack the code and translate the hieroglyphs.

Write like an Egyptian no. 2

Here are some of the Egyptian hieroglyphs. Try to copy them and see how long it would take a scribe to write his records.

A. vulture		M. owl	
B. leg		N. water	
D. hand		P. stool	
F. viper		Q. hill	
G. pot or stand		R. mouth	
CH. rope		S. cloth	
I. reed		T. loaf	
J. serpent		W. chick	
K. basket		Y. reeds	
L. lion		Z. bolt	

Now try to decipher this message—remember it is the "sounds" of some letters that are important, not the spelling!

Awesome Egyptian arithmetic

Intoxicate your teacher with your knowledge of Egyptian arithmetic. Be cool—just drop these facts casually into the conversation.

1 The Egyptians realized that arithmetic was awesome, and encouraged their priests to develop it.

2 Teachers didn't inflict math on everyone, it was a closely guarded secret—as much of science is today. Most of it was taught by word of mouth. If it was written down, it could have been stolen by enemies! (Who'd want it anyway?)

3 The Egyptians used math to solve problems in their building projects. Architects made detailed plans before building began so that every tomb and temple was correctly calculated like ours (see "How to build a pyramid" on page 46.)

4 They used a decimal system like ours, except that zero didn't exist for them.

5 The important Rhind papyrus in the British Museum shows many math problems about rectangles, circles and triangles.

6 The Egyptians used fractions but the numerator, or the top part of the fraction, was always 1. So 3/8 would be written as 1/8 1/8 1/8.

7 Have a look at the Egyptian number chart on the next page. Now see if you can work out how to write these numbers in ancient Egyptian!

14	18	25	30
37	43	56	71
102	175	333	450

8 Test your friends with some Egyptian sums, for example: $\text{III} + \text{III} \cap = \cap \cap$

Egyptian number chart

1	2	3	4	5	6	7	8	9	10
I	II	III	IIII	III I	III III	III III	IIII III	III III III	∩

11	15	22	39	100	1000	10,000
I∩	IIII∩ II	II∩∩	III III III ∩∩∩	⟨	⟨	⟨

Dazzling dimensions

Now try out some Egyptian calculations, and see for yourself how awesome they are.

If an ancient Egyptian asked someone for a hand they probably had some measuring to do! Egyptians used parts of their body, usually their arms and fingers, for measurements.

The width of four fingers, or digits, was called a palm. The length of an arm from fingertip to elbow was called a cubit. Seven palms were supposed to equal one cubit. Check this with your own body. Draw out the length of your arm on a piece of paper. How many of your palms fit along it? Were they right—as far as your body is concerned?

Try measuring a few things around the house—the dog's tail, granddad's inside leg, the length of the kitchen when someone's cooking. Remember, if anyone gets irritated with you, smile sweetly and say it's an educational activity.

Compare your results with those of a tame adult. Any problems? Imagine buying linen for clothes in the market. Who is the lucky one to get sent out shopping, eh? The person with the longest arm in the family, that's who. What you needed was a tall, skinny elder brother.

Well, the Egyptians noticed that they were getting into some awesome difficulties, so they had to invent a royal cubit. This was a standard measurement that was meant to be the same all over the country. It was almost 52.3 centimetres in our metric system.

For longer lengths there was the "rod of cord," 100 cubits, and the "river measure," 4,000 cubits.

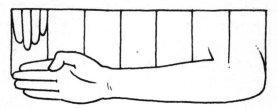

4 digits = 1 palm
7 palms = 1 cubit

Epilogue

Life in Egypt could be hard and cruel. Not many people lived a peaceful life; the mummies couldn't even live a peaceful *afterlife!* But whatever else they were, the Egyptians were truly Awesome. After five thousand years their buildings are still unbelievable for their size.

When Tutankhamun's tomb was opened, the twentieth century world was wildly enthusiastic. The Egyptian "style" was the favourite fashion of the twenties and thirties. Everyone in the world wanted to see his fabulous treasures.

Tutankhamun and the ancient Egyptians became far more famous after their death than they ever were when they lived. For the ancient Egyptians never ruled much more than a corner of their ancient world.

But the people who followed them were *much* more ambitious. They wanted to take over the known world – and a few bits that were hardly known at all. They wanted to rule primitive peoples like the ones who lived in a little group of islands called Britain.

They were even more horrible than the Egyptians. They ate roasted dormice! They were Rotten! The Rotten Romans. But that's another story, and another *Horrible History...*

128

GRISLY QUIZ

**Now find out if you're an awesome
Egyptians expert!**

GRUESOME GODS

Most awesome Egyptian myths have various versions of the same story. Here is one version of the Isis and Osiris story. Sadly, our suffering scribe has scrambled the terrible tale in places! Can you unscramble the words in capitals? (It's easy—about as easy as unscrambling a scrambled egg!)

Osiris was a popular feller—for a king, that is. His people loved him! Of course someone hated him—his brother, Set, who was very up-Set. Slimy Set was jealous of popular Osiris and plotted against him. Set secretly got his brother's measurements and had a **MAGNETIC FIN** casket made to fit. This casket was in the form of a human-shaped box.

Sneaky Set then **IN DOG'S EAR** a large feast. Seedy Set invited Osiris and 72 others. At the height of the **IF IT IS STEVE** Set produced the casket and **ACNE DO NUN** that it would be given to whoever it fitted. All the guests tried the casket for size, but none fitted until finally Osiris stepped into the casket. (What a mug!)

Set (who was not a mug) immediately slammed the lid closed and sealed the casket shut (with boiling lead.) The

SAD LEE coffin was then thrown into the Nile.

Isis was upset at the loss of her husband and **SHE CARED** for the casket all over Egypt. At last she found it where it had come to rest in the roots of a huge tree.

Isis took the coffin back for a proper **ALI RUB**. For safety she hid it in the marshes beside the Nile. Unfortunately for Isis, Set found the casket while he was out hunting and was so **ENRAGED** he chopped the body of Osiris into pieces, and **RESTED CAT** the parts throughout the land of Egypt.

Poor Isis had to then set out again looking for the bits of her husband. At last she found all the parts except one (his naughty bit) and **SMEARS BLEED** Osiris and wrapped him in bandages. The first mummy!

He was also a daddy and his son, Horus, went out to battle his savage uncle Set. After a series of battles neither was able to win. In the end Osiris was made king of the Underworld, Horus king of the living, and Set ruler of the deserts as the god of evil. So they all died happy ever after!

Wrotten Writing

The Egyptians invented writing. They needed it to keep count of all their wealth! They invented the "picture-writing" that we call hieroglyphics.

A. vulture		M. owl	
B. leg		N. water	
D. hand		P. stool	
F. viper		Q. hill	
G. pot or stand		R. mouth	
CH. rope		S. cloth	
I. reed		T. loaf	
J. serpent		W. chick	
K. basket		Y. reeds	
L. lion		Z. bolt	

Now see if you can read this message—remember, the sound of the letters is more important than the English spelling.

POTTY PYRAMIDS

They are H-U-G-E. The pyramids were built as graves for the pharaohs after they left this life. They were filled with goodies so the kings would be as rich in the next life as they were in this life.

Of course they've all been robbed now—some were robbed at the time of the burial and the rest have been cleaned out by greedy treasure hunters in the twentieth century. (They said they were collecting historical material for our education. That's a bit like a bank robber saying his hobby is collecting bank notes . . . they are all just robbers!)

Not everyone agrees the pyramids are graves, of course. Thinking about those great lumps of dense stone, are people with great lumps of dense brain who have other ideas. But which of the following wacky ideas have some people seriously believed? Answer **true** or **false**. . . Someone has said that the pyramids are. . .

1 **Adverts.** The priests wanted to leave something to show the world how great they were.

2 **Simple landmarks.** All maps would be drawn with the pyramids at the centre and distances worked out from there.

3 **Chambers of horrors.** Dead kings were stuck inside, then the Egyptian people were charged two onions an hour to walk around and view their kingly corpses.

4 **Sundials.** The shadow from the Great Pyramid would be used to work out the time.

5 **Fortune-telling machines.** They've been used to predict the birth of Christ, the date of World War I and the end of the world—2979 A.D. if you're worried.

6 **Star calculators.** They help to measure the speed of light, the distances from the Earth to the sun and to keep a record of the movement of the stars.

7 Calendars. They can measure the length of a year to three decimal places.

8 Star maps. The pyramids are laid out in the same pattern as a cluster of stars called Orion. Of course you can only see this pattern if you are ten miles up in the air—or a Martian in a flying saucer.

9 Centres of invisible forces of the universe. Weird things can happen there—like blunt razors turning sharp and people feeling wobbly at the knees when they enter.

10 Calculators. Take the distances around the edges and the angles and whatnot and you can work out the distance around a circle (its circumference) if you know the distance across (its diameter).

Quick Egyptian Quiz

1 The Egyptians made houses from bricks. The bricks were made from mud mixed with straw or something else. What? (Clue: not to be sniffed at)

2 Pilgrims came to ancient Egypt like holiday-makers to Blackpool. What miniature mummies did they buy as souvenirs? (Clue: did they have to kill these creatures nine times?)

3 A weaver who took a day off work would be punished. How? (Clue: you can't beat it)

4 Priests shaved off all their hair and eyebrows. Why? (Clue: not such a lousy idea)

5 Egyptian gods were often pictured with animal heads. Hapy had a baboon's head and Qebehsenuef had a falcon's. But Pharaoh Horemheb was buried with a rare god who had what sort of head? (Clue: flipping tortoise!)

6 The god Khnum created the first Egyptian people. What did the Egyptians believe he made them from? (Clue: they were earthy people)

7 Farmers scattered corn on their fields. How did they trample the seed in so the birds couldn't eat it all? (Clue: they were seen and herd)

8 Another way to keep birds off crops was to use scarecrows. These scarecrows were better than modern ones as they could run around screaming! How? (Clue: you must be kidding)

9 After reigning 30 years a Pharaoh would have to prove his strength. How? (Clue: it was a good idea in the long run)

10 How many sides has an Egyptian pyramid? (Clue: slightly sneaky)

Answers

Gruesome gods: magnificent; organised; festivities; announced; sealed; searched; burial; angered (or enraged!); scattered; reassembled.

Wrotten writing: My nits ar itchy

Potty pyramids: All except **3** have been believed by someone . . . usually someone with more thumbnail than brain, but you can believe them if you like. Most people just admit they are huge tombs for dead kings.

Quick Egyptian quiz:

1) Animal droppings. Poo! Imagine if your house was made of mud mixed with animal droppings! (Maybe it is!) And imagine mixing it in the days before rubber gloves had been invented. The Egyptians also burned animal droppings to make a fire.

2) Mummified cats. The cats had their necks broken, then were wrapped like a pharaoh's mummy. Pilgrims offered the cats to the gods. Vast cemeteries have been discovered with many thousands of these cat burials. It is likely that the animals were specially bred for this purpose. By 1900, hundreds of tonnes of mummified cats had been shipped to Liverpool to be ground up and used as fertilizer.

Horrible Histories note: Some school books tell you the Egyptians turned their cats to mummies because they loved their cute little kitties so much! Nice idea—load of rubbish.

3) He was beaten. Miss a day's work, weaver, and you get fifty lashes. And weaving was a tough job—you worked all day with your knees drawn up to your chest.

4) To keep free of lice. Everyone from Pharaoh to peasant suffered from lice in the hair. Priests became slapheads to keep clean.

5) A turtle. It was not a common statue in Egypt so Horemheb probably had to shell out a lot of money to buy it!

6) Mud. The early Egyptians called themselves "black-landers" because they believed they were made from the dark, rich soil by the Nile River. Khnum, they said, breathed life into them and the mud became human beings. Muddy marvellous!

7) With a herd of sheep, goats or pigs. These herds ran around the field and trampled in the grain. Don't try this at home.

8) They used children as scarecrows. Nowadays we'd probably use traffic wardens because they are scarier than anything.

9) He had to run around his palace. Some historians believe that in the early days of Egypt, if the king failed the test he would be sacrificed. He was literally running for his life!

10) Two. An in-side and an out-side. (Oh, come on! This is a *Horrible Histories* book! What did you expect? A fair question?)

INTERESTING INDEX

Where will you find "blackheads," "Chin wigs,"
"roasted dormice" and "radishes" in an index?
In a *Horrible Histories* book, of course!

Terry Deary was born at a very early age, so long ago he can't remember. But his mother, who was there at the time, says he was born in Sunderland, north-east England, in 1946 – so it's not true that he writes all *Horrible Histories* from memory. At school he was a horrible child only interested in playing football and giving teachers a hard time. His history lessons were so boring and so badly taught, that he learned to loathe the subject. *Horrible Histories* is his revenge.

Martin Brown was born in Melbourne, Australia, on the proper side of the world. Ever since he can remember he's been drawing. His dad used to bring back huge sheets of paper from work and Martin would fill them with doodles and little figures. Then, quite suddenly, with food and water, he grew up, moved to the UK and found work doing what he's always wanted to do: drawing doodles and little figures.

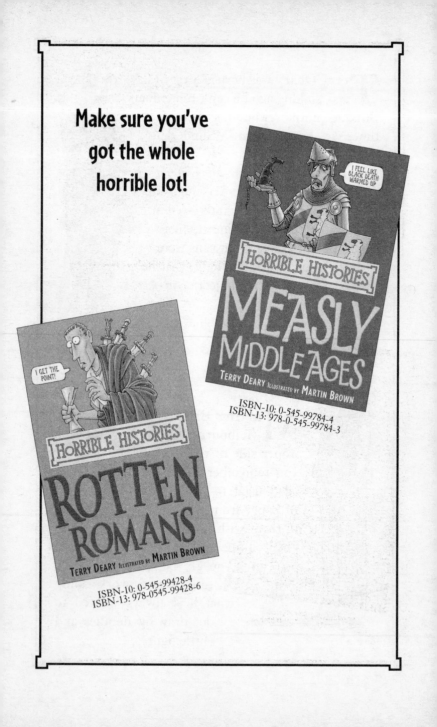

Make sure you've got the whole horrible lot!

ISBN-10: 0-545-99985-5
ISBN-13: 978-0-545-99985-4

ISBN-10: 0-545-99984-7
ISBN-13: 978-0-545-99984-7